Grace All Around Us

Embracing God's Promise in Tragedy and Loss

Stephen Paul Bouman

MINNEAPOLIS

GRACE ALL AROUND US
Embracing God's Promise in Tragedy and Loss

Large-quantity purchases or custom editions of this book are available at a discount from the publisher. For more information, contact the sales department at Augsburg Fortress, Publishers, 1-800-328-4648, or write to: Sales Director, Augsburg Fortress, Publishers, Box 1209, Minneapolis, MN 55440-1209.

Library of Congress Cataloging-in-Publication Data
Bouman, Stephen Paul.
Grace all around us: embracing God's promise in tragedy and loss / by Stephen Paul Bouman.
p. cm. — (Lutheran voices)
Includes bibliographical references and index.
ISBN-13: 978-0-8066-5325-9
ISBN-10: 0-8066-5325-6 (pbk. : alk. paper)
1. September 11 Terrorist Attacks, 2001—Religious aspects—Christianity. 2. September 11 Terrorist Attacks, 2001—Religious aspects—Lutheran Church. 3. Terrorism—Religious aspects—Lutheran Church. 4. Suffering—Religious aspects—Lutheran Church. 5. Loss (Psychology)—Religious aspects—Lutheran Church. I. Title.
BT736.15.B68 2007
248.8'6—dc22 2006037365

Cover design by Dave Meyer; Cover photo © Royalty-Free/Corbis. Used by permission.
Author photo by Kara Flannery.
Book design by Michelle L. N. Cook

The paper used in this publication meets the minimum requirements of American National Standard for Information Sciences—Permanence of Paper for Printed Library Materials, ANSI Z329.48-1984.

Manufactured in the U.S.A.

11 10 09 08 07 1 2 3 4 5 6 7 8 9 10

Contents

1. Grace

New York: September 11, Five Years Later

A Beautiful Fall Morning

On September 10, 2001, our daughter, Rachel, moved into a Manhattan apartment in the shadow of the Queensboro Bridge, with three guys from Dublin, a guy from Paris, and a woman from Omaha, strangers all. On the morning of September 11, she was to go to work downtown at Lutheran Social Services, around the corner from the World Trade Center.

On the morning of September 11, my wife, Janet, headed into New York City from our home in Rockland County, about twenty miles north of the city. She was going to a meeting, also at Lutheran Social Services downtown.

On the morning of September 11 our son Jeremy rose in Jersey City to pack for a noon flight from Kennedy Airport to Nairobi, Kenya. He was going to visit our son Timothy and daughter-in-law Erin who were teachers in Bukoba, Tanzania, on Lake Victoria.

On the morning of September 11, Timothy and Erin woke up to teach their classes at the Kibeta English Medium School. They were anticipating Jeremy's visit which was to include a climb up Mount Kilimanjaro.

I remember driving across the George Washington Bridge early on the morning of September 11 because the sky was so unusually blue, the air warm and clear, the view of the buildings stunning in the bright sunlight. The skyline was moored by the downtown Twin Towers, and I smiled looking at them from the car, as I always did entering the city I have loved for so many years.

Sitting in my office on the sixteenth floor of the Interchurch Center at 120th Street and Riverside Drive, windows looking south, I was meeting with two of my staff. At a little after nine I noticed black smoke rising in the distance. "Jersey," I remember thinking and gave it no more thought. We had lived for eleven years in New Jersey and were familiar with the dirty socks smell of the Turnpike near the airport and of all the lousy Jersey jokes told by the world. The smoke continued to rise in the background as we met. I was getting a little curious when my administrative assistant entered my office. I will never forget the stricken look on her face. "Turn on your radio. Look at the computer. There's been an attack downtown." We all bolted to the window. The towers were wreathed in smoke, black clouds hovering over the harbor cutting through the perfect autumn blue. And so it began.

Like the rest of the world we began to seek out family. Gary Mills of our staff was trying to reach a nephew who was a waiter in the towers, working a breakfast on a high floor. I could not get a call through to Lutheran Social Services but was able to reach a leader in our synod whose law office overlooks New York Harbor downtown. There was no answer at the office of Lars Qualben, a vice president for Marsh McClennan whose office was on the ninety-second floor of Tower Two. My wife called. She was stopped at the George Washington Bridge and was able to make a U-turn and return home. No word from Rachel or Jeremy. A second plane roared down the Hudson, past our office. Our air force scrambling, I thought, not knowing it was headed toward the second tower. Then someone came in and told us that the plane had hit the tower. We watched the buildings fall, the downtown skyline obliterated in smoky ash, enveloping everything.

At noon we met to pray in the chapel of the Interchurch Center. Hundreds gathered. My part was simple. I said Psalm 23 by heart. I invited people to name the names before God of those downtown about whom we were worried, whose fate was unknown to us, as our prayer. My life changed in hearing the names come at me through clenched teeth, strained voices, sobs, shouts. "Rachel, Jeremy, Lars," I muttered.

I called our churches in Manhattan. They were starting to receive refugees from the carnage. I encouraged and prayed with the pastors who were meeting the horror with cold water, open sanctuaries, and listening embrace. The time of lamentations in New York had begun. People began calling to tell their stories of rescue, loss, worry. They gave me names to pray over. Plans for communal prayer, participation in rescue, disaster response began to be formed. At some point I sat down and wrote a brief e-mail to let people know what was happening here in New York. Those periodic online journals became one form of my ministry to others across the country and around the world. Initially they were a way for me to stay steady, to begin to grieve, to let out the feelings, vent the fear. Those journal entries are available online at www.mnys.org.

The phones worked sometimes. Cell phones were especially unreliable. Maybe that's why I haven't heard from Rachel, I prayed. At one point President David Benke of the Atlantic District of the Lutheran Church, Missouri Synod—my partner as Lutheran leader in New York, and dear friend—called. He was stuck in Brooklyn and wanted to know where I could use him. No one could get into Manhattan. I asked him to go to Lutheran Medical Center in Sunset Park, Brooklyn, designated as a primary trauma center. He stayed there into the evening, through the initial rush of wounded, then the long waiting as few came and the horror of the scale of death revealed itself. Mid-afternoon I spoke to the director of Lutheran Social Services. The engine of the first plane fell through the roof of the building of LSS on Park Row around the corner from the towers, igniting a fire. They evacuated everyone in the building—staff, foster children, other clients—and sent them north, joining the soot covered retreat. They arrived safely at St. John's Lutheran Church at Christopher Street in Greenwich Village. I still did not know if our daughter had gone to her meeting in the building which was now burning.

Jeremy called. His trip was canceled. It would be days before any flights entered or left the metropolis. He had walked the few blocks to the river and watched the inferno from the Jersey side of the harbor. He and his fiancé helped those who escaped by boat and made their way back to Jersey City.

Janet called. Rachel had slept in. She was safe. It would be another day before we could get a call through to Tanzania. Timothy told us that Bishop Buberwa and some others had come to their home and prayed with them for his beleaguered city. For days people stopped them on the streets: "*poli sana*," they said. In Swahili: "we are so sorry."

The urge to be home was overwhelming. The rest of the afternoon and early evening was spent on the phone, getting news on what was happening downtown, checking in with many, formulating the beginning of plans that would evolve into Lutheran Disaster Response New York. As the sun descended, I just wanted to hold my wife, Janet. At the entrance ramp for the George Washington Bridge I waited in a line of snarling traffic. A bomb scare had closed the bridge. I saw for the first time what would become a familiar site. People with guns were looking into cars. I drove on the shoulder, showed my clerical collar to someone with a gun and received permission to take a U-turn and return to the city. In the smoky evening I was the only car traveling south on the east side FDR expressway. I got off at 96th Street and drove through empty streets to our apartment where we usually stayed during the week.

I walked to get a slice of pizza and looked down Lexington. Downtown was shrouded in a pillar of smoke and fire of biblical proportions. Weary people were trudging home, eyes glazed. People greeted one another in muted tones. Dazed New Yorkers began telling somber stories. My collar seemed an invitation. People asked for prayer. "Father, will you pray for Vinnie? I don't think he made it." It took me an hour and a half to walk the two blocks back to our apartment.

The walls of the apartment closed in on me. After talking to family members, except Timothy and Erin in Africa, I got in the car and tried again. I just wanted to be home. The bridge was free. I couldn't look downtown. All along the Palisades as I traveled north was the sound of sirens as fire, police, and rescue vehicles rushed south from Hudson Valley cities and towns toward Ground Zero. We were one metropolis that night. Ground Zero was a hole fifty feet deep and fifty miles wide. Shortly after I crossed, they shut down all the bridges and tunnels and locked down Manhattan.

Home. Tears and embraces. Janet and I watched coverage long into the night. We called our pastor and arranged for a prayer service at our church for the next morning. We poured a drink. We prayed. One family in the New York metropolis, repeating what millions experienced around the world.

Endless Day

The long day did not seem to end, sleep was elusive, and in the months ahead, as losses were accounted for, life as we knew it changed irrevocably. War loomed. Endless day as we learned of the forty-seven children in our schools who lost parents. Endless day as we lived through the memorial and burial season, day after day of remembering the dead. Endless day as terror changed the landscape of our metropolis. Endless day as the residue of trauma, depression, anger, grief, sadness, doubt ran through the initial adrenaline rush of response and courage and deep faith, leading to spiritual enervation, a sense of hopelessness. Endless day as the stranger among us became hunted and blamed, as the economic migrants and the poor plunged into deeper poverty in the ruined economic landscape. Endless day. How we longed for the night and true rest.

Rest would come in the midst of the bright and garish day of suffering. Five years later my memories are also about spiritual rest, communal prayer, countless acts of solidarity, kindness, compassion. Rest and refreshment came in hearing Bible stories as if for the first time. As we read the old, old story into our unfolding narrative, Scripture came alive and carried us. Isaiah 62 reminded us that we would be called "a city not forgotten." In Isaiah 58 we grasped our vocation to be the "repairer of the breach, restorer of streets to live in." Baptism took on new meaning when we heard how one of our Lutheran chaplains had run across the Brooklyn Bridge to the towers that morning and anointed with oil the brave fire and rescue personnel who asked for this baptismal reminder as they rushed into the towers and up the smoky stairs. We rested in telling our stories and speaking our pain, encouraged by the opening words of Lamentations: "How lonely sits the city . . ." We saw the heroes in the towers as angels ascending and descending on Jacob's ladder. For a brief time our houses of worship were the most important places in the community and the Bible was a living document of drama encompassing our own.

In the weeks after I would visit each of the eighteen conferences of our synod with only one agenda: how is your soul? The stories which unfolded were a part of the lamentations needed before the beginnings of healing. The week after September 11, President Benke and I had formed Lutheran Disaster Response New York with $15 million sent to us from Lutherans and others around the country and around the world. Through LDRNY we walked with the victims and their families, accompanied the economic victims of this tragedy, provided respite for pastors and teachers, counseling for children, and many other opportunities for comfort and renewal. We formed a bridge with many partners—public, interfaith, ecumenical, private—and nurtured and supported associations for victim's families. I traveled around the country and the world bringing a perspective from the ground in New York to the altered landscape of our world. In places as disparate as Bergen, Norway, the Berlin Film Festival, Kampala, and Bukoba in Africa, and in meetings with Mohammad Abbas and President Katzav in Ramallah and Jerusalem, I was always stunned by how deeply these attacks in America registered in hearts around the world, how wide open the window once was, the opportunity for solidarity which has been squandered.

Interfaith dialogue, communal worship, presence in the firehouses, conducting memorials and funerals, deep conversations about faith and doubt and the presence of God, explaining life on the ground to friends around the world, became part of the fabric of every parish and pastor in our synod.

Several days after the tragedy almost every Lutheran pastor and many lay members of our congregations in our metropolis gathered with our national leaders and President Benke and me at Holy Trinity on the West Side. After visiting Ground Zero with our national leaders I told them: we have been baptized for this moment. My memories, five year later, are about that baptism.

Although I am remembering and telling the story of a small slice of the fabric of the city, the fashioning of spiritual care by the Lutheran religious community and the account on the ground of one bishop, it is also a story with global dimensions, wide presence, and participation. What we experienced and learned in the crucible of 9/11 is relevant to every tragedy. This book is about some of what we learned.

Over these five years I have challenged a Sharia Judge in Ramallah about what Muslim theology and scriptures would have to say about terror in New York; reacted to a World Council of Churches delegation about political lectures while we could still smell our brothers and sisters downtown; led a mass for peace covered by every television network shortly after the war in Iraq began at St. Peter's in Manhattan; participated in planning at Cardinal Egan's office with former mayors Koch and Dinkins the Yankee Stadium prayer service which got my friend David Benke in trouble for his participation. I preached at an interfaith memorial service at Abyssinian Baptist in Harlem, remembering that Dietrich Bonhoeffer had taught catechism there for his friend Adam Clayton Powell. Five years later my memory of that time merges into the anger and witness about life and community, war and peace, today in our changed world.

And of course, 9/11 is about a real Ground Zero, an obscene pile in which people were buried. How often I bristled at the commodification of that horrible time, about 9/11 as a way to talk about politics, or make a point. I felt, for a time, the anger of disenfranchised grief. I would spend time there, and the first time will never leave me. It was days after the attacks. President Benke and I were going there with our national leaders, President Kieschneck and Bishop Anderson, accompanied by chaplains who spent every waking hour there. I was afraid we would be beside the point. But our collars were an invitation. The lamentations, prayers, and tears flowed. I breathed through my mouth under the mask I wore. Stopping and staring into the pile I pictured faces of those I loved, or knew, or imagined the faces of the many names given to me for prayer and remembrance. But here I was without comfort. My mind went blank. I just could not tap into the reservoir of spiritual ballast given to me by church and family and life's experiences. I would always be silent at this place, even today. I numbly stared into this abyss and waited.

Grace

There were three attacks that day, evoking many and similar memories in Washington, D. C., and Pennsylvania. There have been other Ground Zeros these five years, and our Ground Zero experience parallels the violence, fear, helplessness, and vulnerability many in the world experience every day. As I write this, earthquakes rip Indonesia. The South Asian Tsunami, Darfur, and Hurricane Katrina, bombings in Madrid and London, terrorist attacks in which school children perished in Deslan, Russia, are only a few of the Ground Zeroes we have witnessed. Every one of them has jolted me back to that beautiful September day, stirring up in my heart the great longing people felt then to be near us, to stand with us, to do something tangible. In my longing to make a difference in Darfur, to be present in New Orleans in some way, I have been in touch with my own gratitude for the many ways love and grace closed the distance between us in the days after 9/11.

My memories and this book, are a part of a long love story with New York City. I have lived in the New York metropolis my entire ministry. My first call in 1973 was to two congregations in Woodside, Queens, where I learned a little Spanish and directed youth ministry. In 1974 I was called to a congregation in Jackson Heights, Queens, where I served for eight years. This is the neighborhood depicted in the movie *Maria Full of Grace,* the story of a person carrying drugs from Colombia into Queens. Those years we grew a church of many ethnic groups, a typical New York story. In the 1980s I served a parish in Bergen County, New Jersey, while also serving as a consultant to antipoverty community groups throughout New York City. For ten years I have been the bishop of a synod with 230 congregations in Long Island, New York City, and the Hudson Valley—worshiping in twenty-five languages. We have lived in Queens, in Upper East Side Manhattan apartments, Union Square downtown, and now uptown in Harlem. I have always loved the city, but since 9/11 that love has possessed me in ways I can hardly bring to words. In Scripture God's promises and faithfulness are made real in turf, on the ground, in places of hurt and hope. The passion emanating from Ground Zero has become, for me, a kind of Holy Land.

One of my favorite books is *Diary of a Country Priest* by Georges Bernanos. It records the thoughts of an ordinary parish priest, his struggles with the mundane, with his relevance to the rhythm of life in his rural parish, his attempts to pray, his wrestling with faith and doubt. In it he faces his own death even as he has helped others face their own living and dying. The priest loves his turf even while seeing clearly its folly and faults. He loves the people he encounters, even those who vex and irritate him. This book is a kind of "diary of an urban bishop," looking at September 11, 2001, and its wave effects through the eyes of a pastor called to be a bishop, and the struggle between doubt and faith, the effort to pray in the shadow of Ground Zero. It is a journal of awe and respect for the many people whose faith and compassion have left their mark on me. At Ground Zero we learned from others who had gone through tragedy before us, and I pray that some insights we have gained may be helpful to others and relevant to any time of tragedy. These reflections are offered in the spirit of the last words of Bernanos' novel. A parishioner is describing the last words of the dying priest: "He said, 'Does it matter? Grace is all around us.'"

In Every Tragedy: Grace All Around Us

When tragedy strikes, our responses are visceral and spiritual, short and long term, rippling outward. For Christians, liturgy and Scripture and the community of the Body of Christ are deep resources for the responses to tragedy. *Eyewitness, Lamentations, Re-enchantment, Repairers, Visitation, Vocation, Solidarity, Resurrection:* these words etch out grace taking shape all around us in the chaos of tragedy.

The first, visceral response is to be an eyewitness, to tell the story. If we are not present we must put ourselves in a position to hear the story and pass it on. Luke does that in the prologue to his two-part Gospel: gathering and retelling the story of the ministry of Jesus and the birth of the Church. Narrative is the birthplace of meaning and healing. To suffer without a voice is to be spiritually in a dead zone, an object of history, not a subject. Incarnation is God present within history. In my online journal I tell what happened on a beautiful day five years ago in New York—how it was experienced, how people responded.

In tragedy, personal or communal, we often experience a disorientation between the terrible things which happened to us, and the faith and reality we knew before. We can no longer integrate the two. We are cut off from our sources of certainty, comfort, hope, faith. The naming of that space between what was and what has become, between what ought to be and what is, we call "lamentations." The emotion is anger, from the Norse *angr* which means to grieve. Chapter 2 traces the arc of lamentations between the three voices: the one suffering tragedy, the one who listens, the silent voice of God. Lamentations is the eyewitness telling the story again and again and giving voice to the attendant anger, despair, and hopelessness. Building a "house for sorrow" for the eyewitness accounts of a tragedy and their attendant lamentations is a deeply spiritual ministry.

Liturgy helps reorient and integrate the experience of tragedy with the faith, comfort, and hope of the community through history to this present moment. Chapter 3 tells how liturgy and spiritual responses "broke out" in the aftermath of the tragedy. The chapter describes the re-enchantment of the city. The response was visceral: people instinctively prayed together publicly. What was bred in the bone, our spiritual birthright, came out in civic and religious liturgy, song, ritual. Liturgy takes up the ongoing work of lamentations. A third of the Psalms are laments. Liturgy and Scripture undergird the compassionate work of disaster response, propelling the healing work of stepping out into wider worlds of justice and community renewal. As we lament and heal we begin to see connections between what happened to us and the ongoing suffering and tragedy all through history and around the world.

In the following chapters we see how we emerge from tragedy as wounded healers. *Visitation, vocation, compassionate solidarity* are the fruits of Ground Zero, fueled by liturgy and Scripture, connected to each of our stories. God gathers up our lives before the tragedy using what we have experienced and what we have learned—individually and collectively as the church—to help us respond to the immense suffering. God walks with us in healing toward wider worlds of hurt and hope. This book traces the grace of God which is all around us. The grace all around us is abundant life, the presence and promise of our Risen Lord. We know the end of the story, etched out in the details of tragedy and its attendant responses. The grace all around us is eternal.

2. *Lamentations*

"How lonely sits the city that once was full of people! How like a widow she has become . . . is it nothing to you, all who pass by? Look and see if there is any sorrow like my sorrow, which was brought upon me."

—Lamentations 1:1, 12

"What the cutting locust left, the swarming locust has eaten. What the swarming locust left, the hopping locust has eaten, and what the hopping locust left, the destroying locust has eaten. . . . Lament like a virgin dressed in sackcloth for the husband of her youth. . . . The fields are devastated, the ground mourns; for the grain is destroyed, the wine dries up, the oil fails."

—Joel 1:4, 8, 10

Oklahoma City: Mutual Lamentations

On a beautiful sunlit morning Bishop Floyd Schoenhals of the Arkansas Oklahoma Synod of the ELCA and I walked past St. Joseph's Old Cathedral, across the street from the Murrah Center, site of the Oklahoma City tragedy almost ten years earlier. Floyd had reached out to me after the attacks in New York, and I was sustained by his insight and compassion, for he had experienced similar communal devastation. In front of the church was a graceful statue of a weeping Jesus, surrounded by votive candles. Like so many places in New York, this site has become a place for people to focus their grief.

Along the walls of the memorial is a chain link fence, and tucked into it are notes, mementos of love and hope, balloons and other expressions from the hearts of passers by. One of the notes read: "Hello, my name is Chelsea. I am ten years old and I am from New York City. Oklahoma City is always on my heart. P. S. My dad and I are driving from New York to California."

The West and East entrances are framed by "The Gates of Time." Across the top of the gates is this inscription: "*We come here to remember those who were killed, those who survived, and those who were changed forever. May all who leave here know the impact of violence. May this memorial offer comfort, strength, peace, hope, and serenity.*" We entered through the western, "9:03" gate. The exact time of the explosion was at 9:02 A.M. The eastern "9:01" gate represents the innocence of the city before the attack. The "9:03" gate represents the moment the city was changed forever. Before us was the reflecting pool, to our left the field of empty chairs, each one representing someone who died, on the footprint of the bombing site. We walked among the 168 empty chairs, some with flowers, stuffed animals, and other tokens of identity and remembrance.

There is a wall dedicated, by name, to survivors in the immediate impact area. This is a good thing, to formally remember those who were there and survived. Even today, five years after 9/11, people wait for me in the narthex after I have led worship who want to tell me what happened to them on that terrible day, what they saw, how they are doing. I learned in Oklahoma City that even ten years later, folks have not completely "moved on." Healing takes time and shared remembrance and narrative. The time to lament has no statute of limitations.

There is an orchard of trees dedicated to the first responders to the attack. New York City and Oklahoma City both see disturbing trends in mental health issues and suicide rates among those who were first on the scene. First responders exhibiting illnesses from the toxic nature of the disaster site have become a deep political issue. The orchard reminded me of the solidarity of civilians, rescue, police, fire, and other responders in those first hours and days.

Across the street from the Murrah Center was some raw graffiti which reminded me of the primal screams I saw on jagged walls those first days at Ground Zero: *Team 5 4-19-95. We search for the truth. We seek justice. The courts require it. The victims cry for it. And God demands it!*

Inside the museum I read quotes from eyewitnesses and survivors. One reminded me of the beautiful September day in New York City when the towers fell. And then, the most traumatic part of the visit happened. We entered a dimly lit room, a reproduction of the setting of an Oklahoma Water Resources Board hearing room at 9:00 A.M. on April 15, 1995, just across the street from the Murrah Building. I listened to audio of the hearing being conducted. Bureaucrats droned on, papers shuffled, the quotidian sounds of another day at the office. My heart raced, my breathing quickened because I knew that the explosion was about to happen. The waiting was intense and unbearable. Then the sound of the explosion, exactly as recorded, my scream, the room gone black, then the faces of all the dead illuminated in the sudden light. I was shaking as I left that room for a room which draws comparisons with 1995 and September 11, 2001. In front of me was video of a plane crashing into the towers. I let out an expletive, muttered "I can't handle this," and walked briskly out of the building into the sunshine. Bishop Schoenhals and I sit together silently on a bench. We are both crying. This is his second visit. He tells me about the funeral he did for one of the victims. We meditate in silence. It is so good to be together, the memories hard, bearable by being shared. We walk past the empty chairs, through the "9:03" gate toward the changed future.

Lamentations: Building a House for Sorrow

The book of Lamentations begins: "How desolate sits the city that once was full of people. How like a widow she has become." In the ancient world cities were destroyed so often that a literary type emerged called "a lament over a fallen city." What is ancient is modern: New York, Washington, Madrid, London, Beslan, Bombay, New Orleans, Mogadishu, Banda Aceh, Haifa, Beirut. On October 21-23, 2001, Kathleen O'Connor lectured on the Book of Lamentations at Boston University. She said: "This book is 'a house for sorrow,' as Alan Minz aptly calls it." In the lecture she connects the time of Lamentations to the September attacks. "Jews read it on the 9th of AB to commemorate two historic destructions of Jerusalem and their long history of suffering. After September 11, Lamentations belongs to us all."

The destruction of Jerusalem in 587 B.C. was the Ground Zero for ancient Israel. Most scholars place Lamentations in the context of this annihilation, exile, and spiritual devastation. It gathers the many voices of the survivors of the city's fall into a primal scream. The voices are united in pain, insisting on saying what happened and how it feels. To go deeply into the pain and utter it in language is not only soul-crushing work, it is, paradoxically, a beginning of hope and a restoring of the dignity of human agency. It takes three voices to make a lament. There are the voices of the wounded and devastated of Jerusalem, personified in the book as Daughter Zion—bereft, violated, abandoned, widowed. There is the voice of the narrator—the one who listens. There is the voice of God—silent.

If the voice of the Daughter of Zion cannot or will not speak, then grief becomes hopelessness, bitterness, dehumanizing spiritual death. The sufferer becomes an object, not subject of her history. When blunt trauma strikes, denial of pain, strategies of anesthetized disengagement are ways to survive. When the denial becomes routine, when we are stuck in ossified post-traumatic strategies, we become locked in a house of despair, although what we need is a house for sorrow. When tragedy strikes, at some point, we must name it and cry out with its pain.

If the narrator does not show up, then Lamentations cannot be expressed. If the narrator is just a narcissistic voyeur, then the Daughter of Zion is still alone, even with company. But if the narrator is able to be changed, moved to compassion, able to feel his own pain as a birthplace of spiritual solidarity, then two begin to build the house for sorrow.

Hope leaks out in the third of the five poems of Lamentations, but it is only a faint reminder of God's presence and promises. Mostly God's voice is silent. The more insistently those who lament demand God's attention, the louder the silence. Kathleen O'Conner said: "Had the poets of Lamentations given a speech to God, God's words would silence debate. The struggles with pain would come to closure prematurely. Any words from God would trump all speech. Instead, God's silence honors voices of suffering. It gives reverence to anger and resistance, to tears and despair. It lingers over what we in this culture so thoroughly deny."

Two voices in Lamentations weave in and out together throughout the poems, in the context of the silence. The narrator moves from third person observer to first person partner with the Daughter of Zion. At first the narrator impersonally judges: "Jerusalem sinned grievously, so she has become a mockery; all who honored her despise her, for they have seen her nakedness; she herself groans, and turns her face away" (Lamentations 1:8). The one who suffers is an object. The narrator offers his own bogus conclusions (like the friends of Job) usurping God's voice and tacking on his own religious explanations or happy little endings. But the narrator keeps listening, keeps showing up when she cries out: "is it nothing to all you who pass by?" In the listening the narrator stops talking about the Daughter of Zion in the third person and speaks directly to her. "What can I say for you, to what compare you, O daughter Jerusalem? To what can I liken you, that I may comfort you, O virgin daughter Zion?" (Lamentations 2:13). Finally, the narrator is moved to cry out to God *with* the Daughter of Zion. "She," "I," "You," have become "Us," "We." "Remember, O Lord, what has befallen us: look, and see our disgrace! . . . We have become orphans, fatherless. . . . Restore us to yourself, O Lord, that we may be restored; renew our days as of old—unless you have utterly rejected us, and are angry with us beyond measure" (Lamentations 5:1, 3, 21, 22). They feel the pain together, cry out and question together, hurling their lamentations against the silence and waiting on the Lord with the one who cried out, "My God, why?"

The first task in any private or communal tragedy is building the house for sorrow. In eighteen conference meetings I heard pastors and laypeople give voice to their sorrow, their anger, their stories after 9/11. O'Conner said: "Lamentations encourages a religious attitude of openness not to what is beautiful and nourishing in the world, as do so many contemporary spiritualities. It calls us to name, attend to, and to lament what is devastating and brutal, anything that prevents the full flourishing of life on this planet. This is a time to pay reverent attention to every genuine sorrow." People from across the country and around the world took on the ministry of the narrator and listened to us, helping us build the house for our sorrows.

Typically, the world looks away when no longer curious or having achieved a private catharsis. We have already forgotten the South Asian tsunami, and the battered communities and lives in New Orleans and the Gulf Coast since Katrina. They quietly rebuild their lives and face their losses in isolation from a world with a short attention span. Lamentations takes time, sustained attention, loving proximity. When the world says, "move on," incarnation is lifted up as God does not "move on," but "moves in," deeper into the tragedy, in the form of lament. Comfort will come after the lament (Second Isaiah, "you shall be called a city not forgotten . . .)" but for now grace around us is the sound of weeping.

When tragedy strikes us let us pick up our lives and move forward into God's future. But we do not need to avert our eyes from desolation, our own or others, nor let the short attention span of our time move us on too quickly. We can be gentle with one another. Kathleen O'Conner said: "Lamentations is an act of resistance. It teaches us to lament and to become agents in our relationship with God, even if our fidelity only takes the form of telling God and one another our truth. . . . Lamentations crushes false images, smashes syrupy pictures, destroys narrow theologies. It pours cold water upon theologies of a God who prospers us in all things, on a God who cares only about us, on a God who blesses our nation and punishes our enemies, as if we were God's only people."

Our Lamentations are not the isolation and depression of wounded entitlement or private grief, but the community at the foot of the Cross moving outward in solidarity and love toward the sorrow of the world for which Jesus died.

The Knock on the Door: Enabling Genuine Love

For many throughout the world lamentations is part of the fabric of everyday life. About a month after 9/11, I was with a group of local ecumenical leaders at the national headquarters of the Episcopal Church in the United States to welcome an international ecumenical delegation, "A Living Letter of Compassion to U. S. Churches." I serve a church body with a South Asian ministry, a new Batak ministry (Indonesia), an Arab-speaking ministry, many Spanish-speaking ministries, and an East African ministry, so I was pleased to meet Bishop Samuel Azariah of the Church of Pakistan; Dr. Septemmy Lakawa of Indonesia; Jean Zaru of the Society of Friends in Palestine; and Bishop Mvume Dandala of the Methodist Church, South Africa, among others. Their lands know insecurity, violence, and tragedy, and they shared many of their stories. Their presence was crucial. Without the narrator there are no lamentations.

Kathleen O'Connor said: "To honor pain is not an invitation to solipsism, narcissism, or egocentric foolishness. To honor pain means to see it, acknowledge its power, and to enter it as fully and squarely as we can, perhaps in a long spiritual process. To do so is ultimately empowering and enables *genuine love*, *action for others*, and *true worshipfulness*."

When the conversation with our visitors from the World Council of Churches turned political I learned how lamentations enables *genuine love*. I became agitated. I did not want to hear why people hated America or what could possibly justify this mass murder in our city. Not yet. It seemed that these visitors, the "narrator" of Lamentations, were still observing our sorrow in the third-person mode, passing judgment, not really seeing us. I was still lamenting. When it was my turn to speak, I said something like this: "We are just so sad right now. We can still smell our brothers and sisters in the rubble downtown. We are not ready for lectures. Please, just sit down with us and share this time when our faces are in the dust. My head tells me you are probably right and we have a lot to learn and we need a better global politics. My heart is not ready."

I rose to leave. One of the delegation of visitors, Bishop Mvume Dandala of South Africa, asked me to wait. He allowed my lamentations to enable genuine love. This dear, wise man said something like this: "In our culture when tragedy happens we don't all visit at once. We come a few at a time so that each time the person in sorrow has to answer the door and tell the story again of what happened and shed the tears. As the story is told again and again healing can begin. We will keep knocking on the door. We will not leave you alone in your grief."

"We will keep knocking on the door." Genuine love shows up. Cards, letters, visits, money gathered and sent, e-mails, stuffed animals, visits, all of these signs of genuine love sustained us in our lamentations. Genuine love does not say, "it's time to move on" until healing has begun. And genuine love speaks the truth in love, but only what the wounded can bear, sitting down in the dust with the other, silent, listening, speaking a healing word when the Lord gives it.

Five years after 9/11, I suspect, and pray, that we are still answering the door and knocking on the door and telling and hearing our stories. It is a story we share, because it has happened to all of us. And as lamentations enables us to feel genuine love, it will enable our action as wounded healers for others.

Ramallah: Enabling Action for Others

In an upper room in Ramallah about two years ago a Moslem sharia judge helped me to continue to heal from the trauma and loss of 9/11. I was with a delegation of Lutheran church leaders, led by Bishop Mark Hansen, to show support for the Lutheran and ecumenical Christian Church in Palestine, visit their ministries in schools and refugee camps, negotiate with Israeli leaders around the Augusta Victoria Hospital tax issues, and share interfaith and ecumenical conversations. After meeting with several Arab and Israeli political leaders, we walked up several flights of stairs and emerged into the offices of the chief Palestinian judges of the Moslem sharia law. They were dressed in red lined turbans and flowing robes. We sat in a circle and listened to one of the judges address us in Arabic, translated by Bishop Mounib Younan of the Lutheran Church in Palestine. He began by telling the frustration of Muslims who cannot reach the holy places in Jerusalem during the occupation. He gave us historic reasons why the incursion by Sharon on the temple mount was such an offense to Muslims. He cited the Omar Covenant of 638 A.D. in assuring Bishop Younan that Christians would have equal rights with Muslims in the Palestinian constitution. Then he mentioned 9/11.

"We have suffered much because of 9/11," he said. All during this trip my internal antenna was up at every mention of the events of that day. Jews and Muslims, diplomats, political and ecumenical leaders were all using the "since 9/11 everything is changed" mantra in their political analysis and assorted primal screams. I took him on: "I'm from New York, sir. 9/11 isn't just a slogan, a way of talking about politics, or a vessel to fill with your own meaning. It changed our world too, it happened to us. Thousands died, and we are only beginning to feel the pain." I spoke of the misinterpretation of Islam that we were trying to combat, that somehow there was an Islamic justification for this mass murder. "You, sir, are a religious leader, a scholar of Koran, a theologian. We have spent a lot of effort to defend your beautiful religion. I want to know what your scripture, your faith, what you personally have to say about what happened in New York."

He spoke with quavering voice. He said that Islam forbids such killing! It calls us to protect souls and lives. Islamic law leads us to work for one understanding, love, security, peace, dignity. He quoted a sura from the Koran: "The taking of one life is the taking of every life; the saving of one soul is the saving of every soul." He spoke of his hopes for peace and his compassion for the people of New York. I was stunned to silence. I choked back tears. This was the first time I had heard a Moslem leader unequivocally condemn the tragedy of 9/11. He said nothing about why America is hated, or any other rationale. Just, "we condemn." Later a journalist with us said that the Judge must have been waiting to say this to someone. It was direct and primal, from the heart.

Lamentations enabled action for others in two ways. Although New York was heavy on my mind, I was in the Holy Land to help build another house of sorrows. We listened to the laments of Israelis who had endured terror attacks. The shrines, candles, and pictures which sprung up in Union Square helped me enter into the shrines to violence and death at bus stops and markets in Jerusalem. We spoke with many in the West Bank refugee camps who had lost loved ones in the Israeli suppression of the intifada. People took us to rubble and showed us where their families had lived before their homes were destroyed. People invited us into their homes, gave us tea, and spoke of their losses and suffering. It seemed such a small thing to listen but the gratitude expressed to us for taking time and keeping company, I will never forget. And so as both narrator and Daughter of Zion I entered a space where I was able to grow into wider worlds, wider understanding, deeper empathy. I think that this is how it worked for the judge. He knew we were there listening. Maybe our presence as companions to their lamentations opened up space for him to say things he could never say politically in the midst of the conflict. Lament ends the paralysis of sorrow. The defiant act of naming the sorrow is the prelude for action in this world's sorrow in the name of Jesus.

We all must confront our religious traditions, the sorrow they have caused in the past, their possibilities as foundations for building houses of sorrow, even greater habitations for justice, mercy, and love. Islam, Judaism, and Christianity exist in relational or bigoted forms. We must give one another our best, most irenic responses, not the worst or skewed or self-serving responses to this changed world. Israel's president, Arafat, Abbas, and a sharia judge all spoke of the changed world. We were welcome because we were pilgrims for peace, in conversation, listening to the pain and hope in our own hearts, with nothing to give but the wisdom and passion of our sorrow, our faith in the Prince of Peace.

The Hopping Locust: Enabling True Worshipfulness

One year later, on September 11, 2002, I crossed the George Washington Bridge at the exact moment when the first plane hit the towers. The radio played "Lachrymosa" (tears) from Mozart's "Requiem" and my tears mingled with those of the metropolis. Communal lamentations. In that year lamentations took many forms, from silence and tears to tales of death and heroism and rescue, to morbid thoughts about the future, to repeated expressions of abandonment. Sometimes they were enclosed in prayers, other times at the shaking of the fist at God. The question, "Where was God on September 11?" was not only on the cover of *Time*. Lamentations was also taken up in music and liturgy.

The book of Joel sets communal tragedy in the context of lamentations. The first part of Joel seems to talk about a natural tragedy, and the second part about the calamity of exile endured by Israel. It begins with a call to Lamentations: "Hear this, O elders, give ear, all inhabitants of the land! Has such a thing happened in your days, or in the days of your ancestors? Tell your children of it, and let your children tell their children, and their children another generation" (Joel 1:2-3).

A plague of locusts in its inexorable destruction seemed to capture the overwhelming dimension of the tragedy in New York and across the nation. It takes up the relentless, inexorable bad news of New Orleans and Katrina, of the South Asian Tsunami, of the implacable hell in Darfur as well. Day after day new dimensions of the tragedy became apparent. You had a memorial for someone, then you found his jaw. People who were missing were kept alive in the mind during the days of frantic search, then loved ones were asked to deliver DNA as the search became recovery. "What the cutting locust left, the swarming locust has eaten. What the swarming locust left, the hopping locust has eaten, and what the hopping locust left, the destroying locust has eaten" (Joel 1:4).

What made these lamentations such a tragically spiritual event in Joel was that the very means of communion with God and one another were destroyed: the vineyard, the fields, the oil. "Wake up, you drunkards, and weep; and wail, all you wine-drinkers, over the sweet wine, for it is cut off from your mouth. . . . It has laid waste my vines" (Joel 1:5, 7). People who were known to God through manna, and whose very notion of hospitality with one another and God was as companions ("con" "pan" = those with whom we share our bread) via bread had now lost that means of communion. "Lament like a virgin dressed in sack sloth for the husband of her youth. The grain offering and the drink offering are cut off from the house of the Lord" (Joel 1:8, 9). And again, "The fields are devastated, the ground mourns; for the grain is destroyed" (Joel 1:10).

For people for whom oil was the sign of anointing and setting apart holy people and holy things—"thou anointest my head with oil, my cup runneth over"—that means of communication also withered away. "The wine dries up, the oil fails. Be dismayed, you farmers, wail, you vine dressers, over the wheat and the barley; for the crops of the field are ruined. The vine withers, the fig tree droops . . . surely joy withers away among the people" (Joel 1:10-12). Lachrymosa, indeed!

When the carnal things of worship are lost, in the midst of deepest lament in the presence of the divine silence—even there!—we are called to liturgy. "Put on sackcloth and lament, you priests; wail, you ministers of the altar. Come, pass the night in sackcloth, you ministers of my God! Grain offering and drink offering are withheld from the house of your God" (Joel 1:13). Even in the midst of such devastiting loss and lament, Joel tells us that liturgy will comprehend it all.

I lead worship at New Hope, a storefront church near Yankee Stadium. Most of the members are either in recovery or are family members of those living one day at a time. Most are also materially poor. As the congregation began the weekly laying on of hands for healing before Holy Communion, I blurted out to the pastor, "I'm standing in the need of prayer." That week I had received a difficult diagnosis. "For what should we pray," he asked me and I whispered to him my lamentation. The prayer deacons went to the front by the altar. Those asking for prayer and anointing for healing came forward. I knelt with other brothers and sisters. I felt hands on my head. They asked me to speak my pain, and I was able to say, "I'm sick and I'm afraid." Around me others were telling their stories, giving voice to their lamentations. The jazz and Gospel ensemble moved from "Precious Lord, Take My Hand," to "Coney Island Jesus." The room was noisy with tears, the clamor of lamentation, and emotional prayer. The hands on my head were strong, the voices prayed for ten minutes, some in charismatic language I had never heard. They could not take away my diagnosis or all of my fear, but I rested in the community of Jesus and in the promises of God. This prayer and communal lament was brought to the altar with bread and wine, and all was transformed by the presence of Jesus, crucified and risen, at Holy Communion. After that liturgy I was able to begin to face the future, for I had given voice to my sorrow and my fear.

By taking up the loss of bread, wine, and oil, yet calling the people to worship, Joel is telling us that liturgy will build the house of sorrow. Lamentations will enable true worshipfulness. "Yet even now, says the Lord, return to me with all your heart, with fasting, with weeping, with mourning; [the primal scream is prayer!] rend your hearts and not your clothing. Return to the Lord, your God, for he is gracious and merciful, slow to anger, and abounding in steadfast love" (Joel 2:12, 13). Every Eucharist, every Sunday liturgy is placed in the midst of lamentation and hope, of scarcity and abundance.

"Blow the trumpet in Zion; sanctify a fast; call a solemn assembly; gather the people. Sanctify the congregation; assemble the aged; gather the children, even infants at the breast. Let the bridegroom leave his room, and the bride her canopy" (Joel 2:15,16). In this great assembly of those who lament stands those called by the church to lead the worship: pastors, musicians, prayer deacons, all the people at worship. We go from the chancel, where the old, old story is told again to the narthex, where the pastor shakes the hands of those who lament, to the street where tragedy and paralysis await invitation into the house for sorrow. The First Response of the Church in the face of tragedy: Show up. Listen. Tell stories. Pray. Joel's promise: lamentations enables true worshipfulness. "I am sending you grain, wine, and oil, and you will be satisfied" (Joel 2:19). Not now. Not yet in our time of lamentations. But it will come.

3. Re-enchantment

September 11, 2001, Noon

We had watched in horror from our sixteenth floor office windows as both towers lit up, then fell into a cloud of smoke and ash. We are now in the chapel of the Interchurch Center, and I face hundreds who have gathered to pray. For the previous hour we had been doing what millions did in the city, try to track down loved ones working in lower Manhattan. Now the chapel is filled with people not knowing the fate of loved ones, and people who cannot get home as Manhattan is sealed off. In the chapel I asked people to name the folks on their hearts and in their concern.

I heard a changing America and its new history unfold, as the chapel rang out with the precious names of loved ones, spoken through clenched teeth, strained and breaking voices, of workers in Lower Manhattan, fire and police personnel, children in school, friends visiting. "Where's Rachel?" I hurled at God. And in the names I heard our communal movement from security to insecurity; from entitlement to vulnerability; from the veneer of secularity (disenchantment) to a yearning to speak to our Maker; from insularity to solidarity. What has always been just beyond the horizon, bubbling beneath the surface, began to come into view. Everything has changed. Nothing has changed. Everything is connected. Nothing is connected.

Where's Rachel? Where's God? Where's my neighbor? Where is the safe place now? What the hell happened?

Helter-skelter

The great mysteries of existence were staring us in the face. Finitude: falling bodies, endless memorial services. Contingency: I made it out, the guy across the hall didn't; I survived, five guys in my firehouse didn't. Transience: the empty sky downtown. The Bible became relevant, talking about these primal things and the horizon facing all of us: death. In the helter-skelter moments as death rained down, the responses were viscerally spiritual. Sitting next to a soot-covered survivor, screaming hysterically as bodies rain from the sky, a pastor's wife who made it out of Tower One takes her hand and quotes Romans 8: ". . . nothing can separate us from the love of God in Christ Jesus, our Lord." One of our chaplains had run across the Brooklyn Bridge to the towers, anointed with oil firemen rushing into the building—a cruciform reminder of our baptism. Those descending the towers noted the glistening foreheads rushing past them to rescue. Amandus Derr, the pastor of St. Peter's Lutheran Church, heard one of these stories of ascent and descent, rescue and dying, from a member of his congregation. He shared it on Friday, September 14, at a noonday liturgy in their midtown Citicorp location. Hundreds heard him speak of Jacob's ladder, with angels ascending and descending. God is at each end of the ladder, receiving those ascending home, present with those descending here on earth.

On the street outside after that liturgy someone came up to me and asked me to pray for him. He was a Delta pilot and had flown in the first plane allowed to complete its journey into New York after the closing of airspace over the city. He spoke of the fear and sadness besetting pilots and attendants. What had been a good, safe place—the airplane—was now a place of fear and a reminder of brutal tragedy. After my prayer he looked at me and smiled: "You look like you could use a prayer." He then placed his hands on my head and prayed for almost five minutes. That's how it was in those first days, enchantment rippling out, washing over the metropolis, spontaneously, fervently.

At Ground Zero, breathing lightly through my mask, I contemplated the rubble and groped for something, anything I knew, to give me consolation. I stared at the obscene pile, pictures of loved ones buried there. Hearts were broken, but they were broken open. In the helter-skelter of this disaster, Scripture—itself honed in catastrophe and abandonment—came alive and spoke to our inclined collective human heart.

Concentric Circles, Five Years Later

The 9/11 attacks were a boulder thrown in the water, creating ripples that moved out wider and wider. Everything changes; nothing changes—as with all tragedies. From spiritual ripples on the surface, we found religion again: massive public prayer meetings; civic liturgies; increased church attendance; interfaith engagement and estrangement; people urgently seeking meaning. Ground Zero was a hole fifty feet deep and thousands of miles wide in our country.

The political ripples also flowed outward: massive solidarity around the world; then growing repugnance of our unilateral march toward war; an age of terror and hyper-security as the new normal; heightened fear of the stranger; war; global destabilization.

The circles of response to tragedy moved out from the submersed boulder in waves of strategies to deal with trauma and bear the pain: the beginning of the mourner's path; eyewitness stories taking form in a new public canon; the cries of lamentations; pastors, counselors, every citizen running hard and faithfully coping, dealing, serving, improvising. . . . Then the waters became calm. After everything changed . . . nothing changed. On the surface all was as before. These are the rhythms of every tragedy, every loss. Someone we love dies. At the funeral and the few following frenetic weeks there are many visitors, much activity to get affairs in order. Then, months later, no visits, back to normal, and beneath the normal . . . the abyss.

But there is more going on than meets the eye. The calm repose is not the whole story. Percussive waves beneath the surface ripple, still emanate from the boulder in the water and connect wider and deeper than what is visible. The analogy is imperfect but come with me to the deep.

Do not trust the concentric circles you can see on the surface when it seems that a time of renewed spiritual hunger has come and gone. Beneath the surface the tides roll in and go out in cosmic rhythm. Augustine said, "The soul was made for God and will not find its rest until it rests in God." The boulder of the tragedies of our lives plunged into the water does not bring on a new spirituality, but connects with what is already hard-wired into our spiritual DNA, the ebb and flow of the spiritual tide beneath the surface which makes us human.

Do not trust the inevitability of the political ripples which brought momentary global solidarity before the return to the placid water of the political status quo: war, nationalism, religious conflict and schism, the widening gap between the rich and poor. The percussive waves of September 11 yet flow beneath the surface in a spiritual hunger for a more just and compassionate world. There is much more beneath "the clash of civilizations," red and blue state dichotomy. The political vocation to name, bless, nurture, order into harmony is as old as creation.

And do not trust the calm glassy surface of the water, the "normal" way of things after the ripples of dealing with trauma and tragedy subside. Do not trust those who say, "Get over it" "Move on." Beneath the surface, waves of dealing with tragedy are powerful and spiritual. Five years after September 11, 2001, there's still a lot going on beneath the surface. The house for the sorrow of our lamentations is still being built. And all of it is the work of the restless soul seeking God. And that's what we saw breaking out, flowing from beneath the surface on that beautiful September day five years ago.

Drawn to the Light

September 11, late evening: A member of one of our congregations, a part of the massive exodus from Ground Zero through Manhattan, made it safely home to her apartment in the South Bronx. Tired and covered with soot, numb with what she had seen and experienced, she encountered many in her neighborhood. They were sad, puzzled, in shock, like the Emmaus disciples, feeling like the ground beneath them had shifted. She went up to her apartment and got a candle, brought it back to the street and invited her neighbors to join her in prayer. They sang, "Precious Lord, take my hand . . . " They prayed fervently and publicly, as did millions around the world. They gathered every night for two weeks. Those in the neighborhood who went to Ground Zero each day for rescue and recovery told those gathering each night: "Please don't stop doing this. I can stand being down there if I know you are praying for us." Throughout the metropolis and the nation and world the "enchantment" bubbling beneath the surface of life broke forth. Imams, rabbis, bishops, pastors, neighbors, and strangers joined hands and hearts to pray.

We were seeing the manifestation of a turnaround by secularization theorists. From the militantly secular 18th Century Enlightenment through recent times, secularization was viewed as the wave of the future. As the world became more modern (secular), religion would become irrelevant or totally a private affair. Max Weber saw the future as the "disenchantment" of the world. What we saw breaking out around the world on the eve of 9/11 had been going on for a long time, but now was heightened and out in front of us. Nothing is the same. Everything is the same. There is (with the exception of Western Europe) a resurgence of religion around the world, with all the cultural and political consequences attending to it. Samuel Huntington of Harvard examined this reality in his "clash of civilizations" thesis. September 11 turned the light on the "re-enchantment" and "de-secularization" of world history, on the ebb tide of human hunger for spiritual meaning, connection, for holy comfort, for God.

Spaces for enchantment opened up or were revealed in New York, under the harsh light of the September 11 tragedy. We were awash in liturgy and Scripture, in houses of worship and on the streets. The Bible came alive in new ways. Pastor Richard Michel of Trinity Lutheran Church in Staten Island wrote this in the bulletin announcements the Sunday after 9/11: "We now seem to have joined the ranks of those who know 'poverty' in a way we have not experienced it ever before. There have been wars, depressions, and tragedies, but this one somehow is different. Our 'feet of clay' are exposed. We are still reeling from the blow. No matter the cries of our determination to overcome the enemy. This time the blow has staggered us. We shout 'God bless America,' but in the same breath must ask how the loss of thousands of lives can be a blessing. What must God have been thinking? Our humanity calls us. We are a people of great wealth and resources who for a moment have the opportunity to join Lazarus in a beggar's view of the world and learn an incredible lesson from down here—about values and priorities, needs and wants, and how much the rest of the world sees us. The rich man in the parable did not have such an opportunity until it was too late. One scholar calls this view of the world, "the wisdom of the poor." If we can grasp this wisdom, perhaps we will alter our prayer from "God bless America" to "God make America a blessing to all the nations of the world." One can already see the power of Scripture in the percussive waves beneath the surface emanating toward wider worlds and insight.

The classics of art took on new relevance. Bishop H. George Anderson went to Ground Zero with us, then reflected on this experience in a sermon preached September 23, 2001, at the chapel of Trinity Seminary, Columbus, Ohio: "As I saw their faces afterward [rescue workers at Ground Zero] I recalled a fresco by Piero della Francesca depicting the resurrected Christ. From a distance the composition of the fresco is clearly triumphant. Soldiers lie sprawled in the foreground. The risen Christ steps out of the sepulcher, one foot resting on its lid; a banner of victory in one hand forms the apex of the composition. But as you get closer, you notice Christ's eyes—hollow, wary, staring as though they are running recaps of what he has just seen and done. This is truly the face of God, who has overcome evil—not by crushing it, but by enduring it and outliving it."

There were many public and civic gatherings. David Benke prayed in the name of Jesus at a large public prayer service, televised nationally at Yankee Stadium. He spoke of the "field of dreams transformed as a house of prayer." He got in trouble with some in his denomination for praying in an interfaith setting. He wrote on September 28, 2001: "I can only say that the words of my short prayer were only a very public version of what everyone who bears the Name of Christ has been communicating to God every hour of every day since September 11. We have been bruised and buffeted by a great force of destruction. There are times when all of us, especially New Yorkers, have felt as though we have been ground into the dust and the ashes, our lives and dreams gone up in the smoke and the rubble of the Twin Towers. Yet there at our lowest ebb has been Christ and him crucified, humbled beneath our humiliation unto death for the sins of the world, and exalted beyond the highest heaven so that we might rise again here and forever." Then he quoted from the hymn, "Thee will I love, my Strength, my Tower . . ."

We mourned the dead and comforted the living. Two other pastors, a Jesuit priest, and I conducted an ecumenical service of remembrance for the four crews who died in the hijacked planes. It was on September 25 with the employees and staff of American and United Airlines at a church near LaGuardia

Airport. The liturgy continued around the coffee urn and on the street outside the church as hundreds of uniformed airline pilots and staff gave voice to their lamentations.

We prayed ourselves into spiritual solidarity and refocused our collective mission. On September 23, we gathered all the pastors and hundreds of members of our Lutheran churches in the metropolis with our national leaders and regional bishops at Holy Trinity on the West Side. When we sang, "My Lord, What a Morning," we craned our necks to catch a glimpse of the promised new dawn on the edge of our darkness. Prayer, Scripture, sober reflections, music carried us forward.

On December 16, 2001, all of the Lutheran churches in the Bronx gathered for an "Advent Service of Light and Hope" with Mark Hansen, our newly elected national bishop. Many Bronx Lutherans gave testimony to the light, evidence of grace all around us. Mariachi and gospel music, liturgical dance and Scripture illumined hope for the future from the Bronx.

Each time we took visitors to Ground Zero we would stop to pray at St. Paul's Chapel, a haven for volunteers at the site. The walls of the church and surrounding gates were filled with the posters, cards, and other expressions of support from around the world.

Cardinal Egan and I led a liturgy planned by the Black clergy of the Lutheran and Roman Catholic churches in New York, at the Interchurch Center in Manhattan. The occasion was the Martin Luther King day of remembrance. We joined the passion for justice in our city with the lamentations over 9/11.

My staff and I conducted ecumenical and interfaith memorials in our metropolis for Guyanese, Latino, Tamil, Arab, Chinese, and East African victims of 9/11.

Grace, like a rash, broke out after the tragedy, as it does in every disaster. Beneath the placid exterior those waves of spiritual hunger and renewal still run deep.

Havens in a Heartless World

As the late Christopher Lasch wrote about the family as a refuge in a heartless world, many people turned to their local parishes or public liturgies to view their changed world with the eyes of enchantment. As the above list suggests, people flocked to our parishes. They lit candles in public liturgies. Music became an especially potent form of "re-enchantment." Alex Ross, in *The New Yorker* (October 8, 2001), recalls that on May 7, 1915, the day the Lusitania was sunk by a German torpedo, Charles Ives was standing on an elevated train platform when he heard a barrel organ playing "In the Sweet Bye and Bye." One by one, those around him began to sing along: first, a workman with a shovel, then a Wall Street banker in white spats, and finally the entire motley crowd. "They didn't seem to be singing in fun," Ives recalled, "but as a natural outlet for what their feeling had been going through all day long." Ives recorded the experience in an orchestral work titled "From Hanover Square North, at the End of a Tragic Day, the Voice of the People Again Arose."

The collective human heart moved from privatized insularity to the communal side of the horizon and the fullness of human contact in the days after the tragic attack. At Union Square nightly vigils included the lighting of candles, spontaneous singing of "God Bless America" and "Amazing Grace." At Yankee Stadium I joined what was usually a raucous World Series crowd in heartfelt singing of "God Bless America." The New York Philharmonic put together an impromptu performance of Brahms "German Requiem." Bach cantatas and Bruce Springsteen's haunting "My City of Ruin" helped us remember that when words die behind clenched teeth music can shoulder the heaviest part of what we are feeling.

In this chapter I have tried to tell how liturgy and spiritual responses "broke out" in the aftermath of tragedy. The response was visceral: people instinctively prayed, communally and publicly. What was bred in the bone, the tides of our spiritual birthright, came out in percussive waves of civic and religious liturgy, song, ritual. Liturgy and Scripture bind the Christian community and its mission to the presence of God and the grace all around us. Liturgy and Scripture take up the ongoing work of lamentations. Liturgy and Scripture undergird the compassionate mission of the Christian community as it participates in disaster response. Liturgy and Scripture propel the healing work of the Christian witness and presence stepping out into wider worlds of justice and community renewal. As we lament and heal we begin to see connections between what happened to us and the ongoing suffering and tragedy all through history and around the world. Tragedy sets the context for Christian worship and mission. The remainder of this chapter will explore four essential characteristics of this re-enchantment of the spiritual life and witness of the Christian community.

Interfaith

The Christian community must be able to articulate its faith and forge partnerships with many faiths in the global context of today. The towers fell in the name of someone's version of God, and we have emerged from the rubble in troubled and close proximity to believers in many spiritual traditions. A Pakistani Anglican bishop said to me that it's one thing to be a Muslim in Karachi and another in London or New York. We have the opportunity in our setting, where no one faith is absolute, to discover in relationship the most irenic and graceful of our traditions for the common good.

Relevant and contextual

The Christian community must find a language and set of signs and symbols to connect with the many in our society who see themselves as religious but have lost all contact with the traditional forms of the Christian communion. After a tragedy people are hungry to speak to their Maker and willing to give the Christian story another hearing. I spent hours with friends of our children (generation x, post-modern, spiritual searchers) hearing them tell their stories, ask their questions, mourn the loss of friends, grateful for someone identified as a church leader taking the time to listen and share the heat of the day with them. But the forms of the faith they crave are only a distant echo from childhood experiences.

Public

The Christian community must go public. The tragedies of our lives are public. The questions are public. ("Where was God on September 11?" screamed the cover of *Time* magazine). Bogus religious answers are public ("God is punishing us for AIDS," etc.) Accounts of faith traditions are public: "This is not Islam;" "This is how a Christian responds . . ." The church must place its activity in the midst of a world hungering for meaning.

Repairers of the breach

The mission of the Christian community must be Good News for the poor and the stranger. As Bonhoeffer articulated, in a "world come of age," when the forms and traditional language of the church have collapsed there remains the narrow way of Christian discipleship, the way of the cross, of following Jesus to the most vulnerable of this world. It is the inverted pyramid of grace all around us: "Let the one who would be greatest be servant of all." Katrina blew away the curtain of our society. The poor and the black were left behind. After the Oklahoma City bombing the church had to stand with a housing project for the poor and mostly black elderly which was going to be swept away. The hidden economic victims of 9/11 are undocumented, the immigrant, the working poor, children and the elderly, the disabled, the hungry and homeless.

These four characteristics will propel the waves of re-enchantment beneath the surface, bringing hope and healing from tragedy.

Interfaith: The Church in America Is a Church on Mars Hill

This is what the global enchantment of our metropolis looks like: I was at an ecumenical reception for Patriarch Bartholomew at the Greek Orthodox residence on 79th Street. After lunch we spilled out to the sidewalk, looking like the cast from the movie *Men in Black*. I hailed a cab and he stared at me in a black suit and clerical collar and large pectoral cross, and the others on the sidewalk, dressed like they were from central casting.

He said: "Are you from the division of Christianity which follows Jesus?"

I asked: "Are you a Sikh?"

"How did you know that?"

"Your turban, the name Singh, an educated guess. Your Baba of Amritsar was in town last week, right?"

"How did you know that?"

And then he began asking questions. He pulled over and turned off the meter and asked me about Jesus. Just a little respectful knowledge and curiosity about one another opened up this space for enchantment. The common mission situation to which we are called is that of Paul on Mars Hill. There is such a spiritual hunger here, as in the Athens of old, and so many known and unknown gods. Paul respected this hunger and lavish spirituality and engaged it, as we are called to respect and engage it. We have gifts to share.

Each Lord's Day the Lutheran church in the Metropolitan New York Synod, a very small microcosm of the metropolis, worships God in twenty-five languages, and several diverse cultures in English (Liberian, Guyanese, South Asian). The re-enchantment of our country is being carried to us by these immigrant Christians. These ministries in our synod are being done through evangelists, lay leadership, music, powerful preaching, relevant social ministry for people's marginal and vulnerable lives, and they are being done with ecumenical breadth and cultural relevance, which includes interfaith partnerships. This is the very recipe for the explosion of Christianity in Asia, Africa, Latin America—and it's coming to a synod near you.

At a gas station in Queens on December 6: A guy with a turban filled up my car, then handed me a brochure with this quote on the cover: "Recognize ye all human race as one" (Tenth Guru of the Sikhs). On an inner panel was a picture of Balbir Singh Sodhi, "killed on September 15 as a result of mistaken identity." On the back panel is a picture of a little Sikh boy with a turban waving two American flags. This gas station attendant is a neighbor of the church in which we had just met and he is afraid for his life in today's America, but also ready to mix his faith with the various enchantments of his adopted land.

The normal, and biblical, situation of Christians in the world is as a minority in cultural and religious diversity. This is the context of our discipleship. For the first three centuries Christianity lived as a small minority. Outside Europe and the United States, Christianity has always been a minority. The Constantinian experience of Christendom was not the biblical experience. Every word of the New Testament assumes Christians live in a world in which most people do not follow Jesus. The events of 9/11 called forth the deep spiritual particularity of the many diverse communions of our spiritual fabric. We yearned for the best and deepest of our collective soul. For Christians, Jesus and the cross are our guides into the great immensity of this world's enchantment, and the world was open to receive our most truthful expression of community and belief, and to share its own. We keep hearing that this or that is not really Islam, this or that is what it really is. The world is ready to ask as well: What is a Christian?

Relevant and Contextual: A God like Anthony—Telling Stories in a New Language

As I arrived to conduct the memorial service in Queens for a fireman named Anthony, all the streets were blocked by fire engines, uniformed firemen, and police for blocks around the church. The neighborhood was shut down tight. The members and pastor of the modest neighborhood Lutheran church practiced an incredible ministry of hospitality, welcoming hundreds of mourners, including representatives for the governor's and mayor's offices. This modest, faithful parish was suddenly in the public eye, choreographing the rituals of the uniformed services, blending with the liturgy of the church, handling press, protocol, and immense crowds of distraught people. Multiply that picture by thousands during the season of funerals.

In his sermon the pastor talked about "A God like Anthony." A brave, baptized child of God was remembered. He had finished his shift at Ladder 35 on the West Side on the morning of September 11 and was on his way home when the first plane hit the World Trade Center. He was buried in the act of rescue. Many in the church were not accustomed to being in church. The conference pastors and lay members of the congregation joined the parish pastor and me as we sang the liturgy on behalf of those who did not know the words or were too numb with grief to sing. In that tableau is precisely the context and theological task of the church.

For liturgies and ministries of encounter with this world seeking enchantment we have been ordained and baptized. The preacher was inventing a language of engagement in which to tell the old, old story. The preacher moved from Anthony who died in the act of rescue to God, whose rescue of the world from sin, death, and the evil one was accomplished at the cross and the life laid down for others.

There are two important Greek words in the prologue to the Gospel of Luke, chapter 1:1-4. Luke speaks of his desire to write an ordered account of the life, ministry, and teaching of Jesus. The first is *parédosan*, as in "just as they were handed on to us by those who from the beginning were eyewitnesses . . ." The Greek *paradosis* means something like "handed on" or "handed down," as in the baptismal dress or the Yankee sweatshirt. The *paradosis* is the tradition from Adam and Eve to Paul and Priscilla to today, which sums up the continuity of God's salvation. The great "hand-me-down" of the Gospel moves all our waiting, searching, lamenting moments into the stream of biblical faith, the journey of all God's people. Our baptismal incorporation into this journey of faith gives depth and content to our longing for faith. After a tragedy, people will not be satisfied connecting to the thin air of wishful thinking or spiritual bromides. The tradition of the Gospel is the promise of God to love us unconditionally through the death and resurrection of Jesus. This *paradosis* is conveyed through the power of the Holy Spirit in the re-enchantment of Word and Sacraments. So then, the memorial liturgy for Anthony was *paradosis*, and the hundreds gathered, who may not know the words or the story or the arcane insider language of the church, were yet in the company and within hearing of the great "hand-me-down" of the cross and resurrection of Jesus, the grace all around us.

The second word is *as pha'leain*, as in "that you may know the truth (or have assurance) concerning the things of which you have been instructed." It names what we are waiting for in faith, what the dazed survivor of tragedy seeks. *Asphalia* doesn't mean clinical proof, or a strangely warmed heart, but something more like assurance or comfort. *Asphalia.* As in that old hymn, "Blessed *asphalia*, Jesus is mine." *Asphalia* is the pastoral and missionary art needed today: to connect the old, old story with a public bereft of the language of the church; to bring together *paradosis* and *asphalia*. This assurance and comfort is based on the great hand-me-down scriptural story of Israel, Jesus, the birth of the church, reaching back to Abraham, Sarah, and Hagar, centering in the womb of Mary, exploding through the power and preaching of the church in the Spirit to Jerusalem, Samaria, Rome, and even the streets of Queens and its grieving hearts. *Asphalia* is the dependence of the believer, not on the events of the proximate moment, rational understanding, correct prayer, pat answers, or anything else but this: that the dying and rising Christ lives for us eternally and is with us in every waiting, lamenting, seeking moment. Romans 8, "nothing can separate us from the love of Christ," is not about coping, but about seeing in all things the grace around us.

Anthony's father got caught in the eulogy. He was animated, pensive, but fully engaged as he mentioned one memory after another, but he could not get out of the cul-de-sac of memory and bring it to a close. On and on he went, because every time he began to wind it up he was unable to face the terrible truth. Anthony is dead.

Pastor Bruce Modahl of Grace Lutheran Church in River Forest, Illinois, preached a funeral sermon in which he spoke of the "eu" words. *Eulogy* is about the past. *Euphemism* is about sugar-coating the truth. "Anthony will be with us every time his children smile." The church leads the world to another *eu* word because the church is a truthful community following the One who is the way, the truth, and the life.

At the table at the Eucharist the truth is declared, the world's narrative is told, and promises are entertained. *Christ has died.* Anthony has died. We say it and face it. *Christ has risen.* Anthony has been buried with Christ by baptism into death, so that just as Christ was raised from the dead by the power of the Father, so, too, Anthony will walk in newness of life. *Christ will come again.* And bring us home where Anthony awaits, "with angels and archangels and all the company of heaven . . . in every time and every place."

Here, then, is a parable for the mission of the church moving forward. Hundreds show up for worship not knowing the words to the liturgy or the details of the story, but with a raw sorrow and hope. They bring childhood memories, passages like Psalm 23 and the Lord's Prayer learned by heart, or the fading memory of church-going parents. The faithful remnant of the congregation gathers to sing the liturgy for them. The preacher invents a language to engage them . . . "A God like Anthony." And then signs and symbols connect *asphalia* to hearts longing for a story to get them through the night. They lined up and came forward with outstretched hands. You could see it in their eyes as they approached: the hope, the doubt, the sorrow, the anger, the reverence, the faith. Bread connects, a tactile and carnal assurance.

In the weeks after September 11, I visited each of our eighteen conferences, did one-on-ones with over two hundred pastors, and in the evenings met with many lay leaders, telling one another stories. There is no Gospel comfort without the opportunity to voice our laments, our eulogies, our questions, our stories of rescue, guilt, contingency, transience, and death. Pastors have put on their collars and walked the streets, and they have been the recipients of these stories. I believe that the primary ministry of the baptized in the world will be public, placing themselves on the Emmaus road and encouraging the telling of the stories. The hem of the garment of Christ's presence has to be out there in the open, available to those longing to touch it. We can connect these stories to The Story and allow our world to be shaped by it.

Two months after Anthony's memorial service they found his remains. His father and brother were on the FDNY detail which recovered his body. They lifted him personally from the wreckage and carried him out. The day after I learned this I attended a Good Friday liturgy at St. Peter's in Manhattan, which centered on Bach's "St. Matthew's Passion." The words of Anthony's pastor were seared into my heart as I listened to this part of the Passion: "I thought of that beautiful aria in the St. Matthew Passion, when Joseph of Arimathea lifts the body of Jesus: '*Mache dich, mein herze rein\ich will Jesu selbst begraben*.' (Make my heart clean. I will grasp Jesus to myself.) The church was filled to overflowing that Good Friday after 9/11 in New York and when the congregation sang "Lord let at last thine angels come" we had experienced the core of our faith and hope as Christian people. In that faith we could experience, even at a recovery at Ground Zero, the grace all around us.

"No, I have not lost my faith." The expression "to lose one's faith," as one might a purse or a ring of keys, has always seemed to me rather foolish. It must be one of those sayings of the bourgeois piety, a legacy of those wretched priests of the eighteenth century who talked so much. Faith is not a thing one "loses," we merely cease to shape our lives by it." (Georges Bernanos, *Diary of a Country Priest* [New York: Carroll & Graf Publishers, 2002])

Public: For the Life of the World

Mr. Kim survived two brutal wars in his mother country, Korea. But he did not survive an encounter with a mugger in the hallway of his apartment in his adopted country. His stabbed body ended its earthly journey at the age of eighty. Mr. Kim and his family were members of the congregation I served in Jackson Heights, Queens. The casket was set up like a Shinto shrine, with pictures of the deceased, flowers, and two posters with Korean ideograms. One poster gave biographical details. The other held Psalm 23.

After the funeral a motorcade of forty cars wended its way to the cemetery. After the graveside committal each family member bowed low before the casket in deference to another ancestor, the communion of saints. Then something remarkable happened. The entire funeral party began walking from the grave, but not to their cars. They filed over to a nearby grove of trees, spread out blankets, food and drink, and had a picnic. One of the family members came over to me and smiled, handing me a sandwich and a soft drink. "Eat and drink, pastor, enjoy! Life goes on!" And so it did, as we ate and drank among the tombstones, celebrating life in the place of the dead transformed. The elementary act of eating and drinking in the graveyard was sacramental, communion with the God of creation.

The public context of Ground Zero and every tragedy will be lurking at every liturgy and act of the church. To place the eucharist in the midst of the world at Ground Zero is not to baptize life with extraneous dousings of God. It rather recognizes the presence of the incarnate Lord in everything. The carnal vessels of water, bread, and wine, eating and drinking, root the grace of God in the things of this world. We cannot spiritualize away the concrete context of God's love for the world any more than we can spiritualize out of existence the loved ones we could still smell buried at Ground Zero.

Enduring tragedy can move us from private to public religion. When the towers fell we were able to gather the interfaith leaders of the metropolis because we were already a public church. After an African immigrant was killed by police in a hail of forty-one bullets at his Bronx doorstep we realized that we were a disparate and diffuse collection of enchantments, out of relationship with one another and the public square. We organized as the Conference of Religious Leaders, began telling our stories to one another, and entered the public arena, culminating in a historic prayer service for racial justice at St. Patrick's Cathedral several years before 9/11.

Parishes which had already "re-rooted" in their communities were already known as places of refuge for the community. Pastors who knew their turf were already at home in the local firehouses, police stations, businesses, already relevant to local public officials and community groups—parts of church-based community organizations which had built Nehemiah housing, gained jobs and economic development for their communities. The public church must emerge from every tragedy—yet it will remain private if it is not already public before tragedy strikes.

Looming over it all is the cross of Jesus, a public execution, where a public narrative was being told among Jesus and the thieves, where this great public act of love prompted the centurion to say "surely this one is the Son of God." Where the cross is raised, God draws all humanity to God and to one another, and the faith of the centurion is recreated.

Repairers of the Breach: The Church as God's Gift to the Poor and the Stranger

Our context for ministry will continue to be a world in which most of the people live at the edge of survival, and the legacy of 9/11 in our country will continue to be economic hardship and increased hunger and homelessness. Pressure on immigrants, asylum seekers, and the "stranger among us" will increase. It is estimated that over two hundred people who died on September 11 were the only ones with documents in their families, leaving those they sponsored (and thousands of other undocumented neighbors) without networks of support. We need some real help here from our theologians to help us see the Bible as God's love letter to those who are poor, oppressed, despised, hated, beside the point. Even in our own churches, ministries to and with the poor are usually the road not taken by seminaries, candidates, programs, initiatives, resources. The massive and wonderful effort by the whole world to be at Ground Zero in person, prayer, and support magnifies the sadness of the Ground Zeros we have missed: the continuing Ground Zero of AIDS, of spending more money for jails than education, the twenty million American children who go to bed hungry every night, the genocide in Darfur, the misery and hunger which fuels economic migration from south to north. We are seduced by fear into elevating questions of security over welcoming the stranger, standing with the poor. The only way to ultimate security is the death and resurrection of Jesus. The only way to security in this world is through the well-being of every child of God.

People are giving the church another hearing these days. What does your faith community look like? What is a Christian? Jimmy Carter told us, at a Habitat for Humanity meeting in preparation for a project in Harlem, that the hardest thing to do in this world is for a person of privilege and a person in poverty to be in the same room together. Can the church show the world communities which live the eucharistic promise that everyone eats together? Do we have the same urgency as the response to Ground Zero, the same resolve to lift up the gifts of people in poverty and offer communities to the world which anticipate the promise of the eucharist: "Christ has died, Christ is risen, Christ will come again"?

I end this chapter of re-enchantment with a story from my last parish ministry in New Jersey. It haunts and inspires me to this day, and reminds me of the unlikely places of enchantment where God is present in grace all around us in the sacrament of the poor.

Edgar is, by anybody's standards, a strange character. He lived alone in a welfare motel near our congregation. For some reason he adopted our church and walked two miles to the liturgy. He seemed a good man with a true and honest faith, if a bit rough around the edges. He could come across kind of scary, which happens when social graces get rubbed off in surviving an inhospitable world. He would interrupt the sermon from time to time—"oh, you don't mean that!"—and I would ask him to chill. But he knew his confirmation verse by heart and when he grasped the bread at communion it was as if he was being handed the Hope Diamond. Truth be told my heart sank on Palm Sunday when he was waiting in the sanctuary for me after a full day of liturgies, first communions, and pastoral conversations. I knew that when Edgar waited for me he wanted a ride, time, money, conversation, fragments of his survival.

I wanted to go home, but we went out, two by two, just as Jesus sent out the seventy in Luke's Gospel. On the ride to his motel he talked my ear off, critiqued the sermon. I prayed for patience. Yet something strange and wonderful began to occur as I pulled into the parking lot of the run-down motel, Ground Zero for poverty in this land of plenty. A door opened and re-enchantment began to emerge. Out came an elderly woman. She knocked on another door and another elderly woman appeared. They limped toward our car and others waiting on the edges followed. They had been waiting for us. I was in someone else's church now. Mothers with children clutching their hands, people with vacant eyes in various stages of coherence, elderly and infirm with canes and walkers, they came to the car. For the first time I noticed that Edgar's hand grasped a bunch of palms. The first lady was by the door. Edgar gave her a palm branch and she clutched her piece of palm like a life raft. I could only watch in reverent awe as the palm branches were distributed in that graveyard in the shadow of the George Washington Bridge.

Edgar was the only person who had ever passed for a pastor in this backwater parish of broken souls. I tell you, there could be no more fertile soil for "church growth" than this concrete parking lot and its children of God awaiting the enchantment of grace.

"Bless us!" he commanded me. I got out of the car, blessed their palms . . . "Hosanna, blessed are they who come in the name of the Lord!" . . . placed my hands on each forehead and pronounced the benediction. If I would have had bread and wine I would have fed them right there. Re-enchantment emerging from our various tragedies must have something to do with turning our church's life—a life rich in liturgical faithfulness, beautiful music and the arts, Scripture seriousness, evangelical fervor, confessional integrity—toward a motel of burnouts and the deep corporal and spiritual needs shared by all humanity at Ground Zero.

These words, then, between us as we go two by two where we have been sent, in the midst of the enchanted graveyard and the rubble of grace around the Ground Zeros of our tragedies: The Lord be with you. . . . Lift up your hearts. . . . Let us give thanks to the Lord our God. Christ has died. Christ is risen. Christ will come again.

4. Repairers of the Breach

"You shall be called repairers of the breach, restorers of streets to live in."

—Isaiah 58:14

"He has . . . lifted up the lowly; he has filled the hungry with good things."

—Luke 1:53 The Magnificat

Strangers on the Road: Repairers of the Breach

Here is the face of tragedy. Two friends are walking home on the eve of the great tragedy. They are dazed, their conversation registers disbelief as they nod their heads in shock, talking about the loss of their friend, their integration of faith and life, of history and hope. Their world was so upside down that they did not recognize the stranger joining them on the road of sorrow. They cannot yet see resurrection looming over this tragic Friday. The stranger does not confront them, but instead draws them out. "What were you talking about? What things happened in Jerusalem today?" They pour out their lament to the stranger. They arrive home and invite the stranger to enter. Word and bread and wine and the presence of the stranger eventually set their broken hearts aflame. They recognize resurrection. The Risen Lord is the bottom line.

The boulder of tragedy plunges into the water. Calvary. The cross. First we must attend to the concentric ripples on the surface. We must deal with what we can see. We must join the dazed friends on the road and show up not where we want them to be, but where they are. We must draw them out—what things did you see, hear, feel, lose? We must attend to their immediate material and psychic needs. We must begin to respond to their despondent spirits. It takes time. We must not try to get them back on the faith too soon, we must not dance in the sunshine while they are in the cave. At the end of the mourner's path is God, as the psalmist has promised: "Where can I go from your spirit? . . . If I make my bed in Sheol, you are there" (Psalm 139:7-8). Always present is the Word, the narrative of faith; bread and wine; prayer and liturgy, objective reality not dependent on how we feel today. As we continue to show up, to attend to the sorrow, to comfort and heal and renew, the face of the Stranger slowly becomes familiar. Grace comes into view. Resurrection beckons. This is a marathon, not a sprint. You can't force hope, only experience it in God's good time. Sometimes you walk the path in both roles: comforting stranger who shows up on the road and, dazed and wounded mourner on the eve of the tragedy, trying to find his way home. In Galatians Paul gives insight into this dual role of caregiver and receiver. "Bear one another's burdens, and in this way you will fulfill the law of Christ . . . for all must carry their own loads" (Galatians 6:2, 5). Carry your own load. No one has the right in the Christian community to expect to have their burdens borne as entitlement. Yet when others carry our burdens, it comes as grace: refreshing and unconditional.

That is the outline of disaster response. Show up. Attend first to the ripples on the surface. Accompany the pain on the road. Respond, rescue, reach out, call, pray, touch, embrace, feed, shelter, cry, reassure. Stay in touch with the resources of faith and keep the fires of hope burning, even if there seems no possibility of comprehension or integration of experience and spiritual hope. Strangers begin to join us on the road: those who have experienced these things before; those whose vocations are to respond and rescue and organize. Experience, empathy, resources, grounded faith join us on the road, walking with us until we can experience and reclaim those gifts from our own wounded midst. Then organize for the long haul. Gather resources. Work with existing networks in the public, private, and non-profit arenas. Strengthen the mediating institutions of church, congregation, community, and family for the long journey ahead. Tell the stories, lift up the heroes. Do communal exegesis, working with the faith community toward spiritual meaning, resurrection, hope, in recognition of the grace all around us. Be moved outward by the tragedy to work toward justice in the wider world and the public arena. Whether it is a community, a denomination, a congregation, a family, or an individual facing tragedy, this is the rhythm of response.

"The Lord will guide you continually, and satisfy your needs in parched places, and make your bones strong; and you shall be like a watered garden, like a spring of water, whose waters never fail. Your ancient ruins shall be rebuilt; you shall raise up the foundations of many generations; you shall be called the repairer of the breach, the restorer of things to live in" (Isaiah 58:11-14).

It takes time. Isaiah 58 offers powerful words of hope and resurrection to the ruined city. But remember that the city was ruined, occasioning the bitter and angry Lamentations many centuries before these words: "How lonely sits the city that was once full of people! How like a widow she has become . . . is it nothing to all you who pass by?" (Lamentations 1:1, 12). The demand that all those who pass by, and that God pay attention was a lament carried on from generation to generation. Only now, in this passage, is the beginning of the healing response. The author of this text addresses the community of Israel who had returned from exile in Babylon. The message joins the community in their concern to rebuild the walls and the ruined streets of a ravished Jerusalem and surrounding neighborhoods. They are also concerned with rebuilding faithful commitment to worship and ethical life of the covenant. "You shall raise up the foundation of many generations" (Isaiah 58:12).

Every tragedy calls the question on our priorities, the strength of our communities, the depth of our spiritual resolve to be "repairers of the breach, restorers of streets to live in." Lamentations attends to the ripples of sorrow, anger, shock, human need emanating forth from the impact of the boulder. "Repairer of the breach" is the long-term ministry which rides the percussive waves beneath the surface—justice, renewal, communal solidarity, the well-being of every child of God.

The burning question of the writer of this text is whether the communities and the nations that join them are worthy to stand in unity and justice when God appears and Zion is restored. Can Israel's people standing before the breach of their ruined community—the hungry, the ruined streets, the naked, the homeless poor, the afflicted—while pointing the angry finger at one another, be fully servants of God?

Calls and Letters

When disaster strikes you get a lot of calls and advice. The best advice I got was from a North Dakota bishop who had led in setting up response to the flooding in the Red River Valley, a tragedy in which churches and homes were destroyed, life was lost, and economic devastation was deep and lingering. "This is not a time to ask permission, get opinions, consensus. Help the people immediately. Spend the money you need to spend. Your pastors and people need you now. The city needs a strong church responding vigorously. Be a leader. You are doing this for all of us. Count on us. We are in this together."

His check was one of the first, thousands of dollars from the churches of his synod to be used at my discretion. His call was presence on the road, reminding me that we were not the first to experience tragedy, that a body of knowledge and resilient experience was ready to join us. His council of boldness, pushing my body toward the road, strengthened my weak knees and shattered resolve. His show of material support pointed me to trust in God's abundance in a time and ethos of scarcity and spiritual doubt. He helped me find the focus of my unfolding ministry: care for caregivers, servant to the church, leader in the community. We can do this for one another.

An e-mail from a member of one of our Long Island congregations two days after 9/11: "I ask that my husband (a member of local 3-IBEW) be added to your prayer list. He was assigned by his union to work at the World Financial Center for Merrill Lynch . . . he ran outside of the building only to see, as he described it, the second plane crash and dozens of people jumping to their death . . . the experience has had quite an impact on him and his sleep patterns . . . one of his co-workers died."

There were many e-mails like that. People expected me to keep a list, encourage a ministry of prayer. Strangers on the road needed company. It becomes the work of leadership in the community of Jesus to place the fringe of the garment of the church on the road where those reaching out for consolation and connection can touch it. In my online journal I asked for the stories, the account of the losses. We collected the names, prayed frequently and fervently for these dear faces known to us even as we prayed for all affected by the tragedy. The Lutheran Counseling Center had a toll-free number available to the public several hours after the downtown attacks. It logged thousands of calls a day, another fringe of the garment of Jesus on the road.

The morning after the attacks David Benke and I received two calls from the national leaders of Lutheran Disaster Response. Similar calls went out to leaders in New York from Methodist (UMCOR), Episcopalian, and other ecumenical disaster networks. It was like the cavalry arriving for rescue. They walked with us every day for over a year, bringing us resources, wisdom, and organization. Soon human and material resources began to pour into New York. God does not leave us alone on the road.

An early phone call on the first Sunday after the attacks from our daughter, Rachel: "Dad, I'm outside the church and

I'm afraid to go in. It's my first time teaching Sunday School. What will I say to the children? I don't know what to tell them." She was every person of faith in our metropolis on that Sunday morning. I told her to go in and just be with the children. They needed her to be herself, whatever she was feeling or able to say. They needed to be loved, heard, touched. They needed the company of their elders. I wanted to reach through the phone and hold her, this child of mine dazed on the road. Although September 11 wounded all of us, we were yet called to be present and speak a healing word to our wounded communities and the world. "Bear one another's burdens . . . each carry her own load." In a time of few words Rachel would be in the company of objective things: the faithful community, bread and wine and Word conveying God's promises, the resilience of children. The children would probably not remember a word she said to them, but they would remember and draw comfort from her presence.

Letters, e-mails, cards, phone calls from around the world and across the country reminded me that the wave effects of this tragedy went beyond the three places where the planes fell. The bishop of the Lutheran Church of Jordan and Palestine was traveling in the country. He came to New York and we shared breakfast a few weeks after the attacks. He prayed with me and listened to me. He shared his experiences of terror, occupation, attack, and suffering. He helped me to claim a ministry of peacemaking and interfaith engagement as a response to tragedy. Cards, letters, breakfast prayers, grace all around us as we walked the Emmaus road from Ground Zero.

Lutheran Disaster Response New York (LDRNY)

Lutheran Disaster Response New York was born on the day that we first went to Ground Zero. We went with our national leaders, arranged by one of our pastors, Steve Unger, an FBI chaplain who had spent every day at the site since the attacks.

His briefing revealed the horrific suffering and death, as well as the depth of faith that made his presence an oasis of grace. All of downtown was inaccessible to the public and we rode down in police cars. The West Side Highway and contiguous streets were lined with people holding signs of gratitude and cheering every police, fire, and rescue vehicle—a kind of Palm Sunday entry into the city. At Ground Zero I breathed through my mouth to avoid smelling my brothers and sisters. We arrived from Ground Zero to the services at Holy Trinity on the West Side, the first gathering of the Lutheran community since the attacks. The area was filled to overflowing and we spent many hours with individual pastors and parishioners as well. Standing with Presidents Benke and Kieschneck and Bishop Anderson as we all sang, "My Lord, What a Morning," I was grateful for those standing with us, and by the resurrection promise of the faith we shared.

That evening, when David Benke and I had one synapse left working in our brains, we met in the sacristy at Holy Trinity with our national bishops and leaders of Lutheran Disaster Response, and formed Lutheran Disaster Response New York. We engaged John Scibilia as coordinator. John is a New Yorker who was Director of Schools for the ELCA at the time. David and I agreed to do this ministry as the church. All were welcome to help; he and I would lead this ministry and sign every check. The response was magnificent. Over the next days millions of dollars came to New York from our national church bodies and fraternal organizations.

We hit a routine, of sorts, after the cathartic reunion of the Lutheran family in New York with its regional bishops and national leaders, the pilgrimage to Ground Zero, and the memorial services that had begun. David and I spoke almost daily with local and national leaders in disaster response. We set up a system of respite for pastors and lay leaders under the leadership of Pastor Cherlyne Beck of my staff. Our leaders were running hard, but we were ready when they began to crash. Listening visits to pastors and leaders in each of our conferences continued.

Funerals and memorial services continued. Our offices became an unofficial headquarters for the many disaster response efforts in the city. FEMA, New York Disaster Interfaith, ecumenical partners began to form durable coalitions. John Scibilia placed Lutheran Disaster Response New York in the middle of the networking. We became what we still are today: a bridge and umbrella helping coordinate an incredible array of alliances and programs. Lutheran Social Services set up shop in our offices. People began to drop by with gifts. Our office was a menagerie of stuffed animals for the kids in our schools, forty-seven of whom lost parents. Leaders from Aid Association for Lutherans and Lutheran Brotherhood presented checks of over $8 million dollars.

LDRNY became a table at which social ministry organizations, congregations, synods and national church bodies, ecumenical and interfaith partners, private and public agencies could be woven together in a ministry called "Comfort and Renew."

We learned from others. Those who responded at Columbine helped us begin our day camps for children in New York. Those who responded in the floods of the Red River Valley sat with our pastors in New York.

Beneath the necessary organizational structure and fiscal accountability (all disaster efforts were under intense scrutiny) there was human comfort. LDRNY was "in the breach" comforting school children, assisting families who lost a loved one, giving direction toward new employment to the jobless. Immigrants were given new opportunities. Church workers found respite. Five years later LDRNY continues to be a thousand stories of love on the move, the legs we put on our prayers.

Among the many ministries beneath the LDRNY umbrella are these:

Project Life (Lutheran Initiative for Empowerment) is a case management program coordinated by Lutheran Social Services to help 9/11 economic victims access the myriad sources of help and benefits available, and connect them with the right services. There is a concerted effort being made to include those who are most vulnerable or left out: undocumented immigrants, limo drivers, hotel domestics, window washers, venders (the operator of a food truck destroyed outside one of the towers is a Honduran from one of our congregations who was supporting ten people back home), the recently unemployed, and others. Case managers speak Mandarin, Arabic, Spanish, and Fujianese as well as English, and they have maintained over one thousand in the system. We are walking with hundreds of people, from immediate assistance (rent, food, gap funding) to long range plans for new beginnings. LDRNY organized an "Unmet Needs Table" which brings together many case management programs with funding sources and NYDIS (the New York Disaster Interfaith Services).

Counseling: The Lutheran Counseling Center set up a toll-free hotline on September 12. Thousands have used it. Trauma counseling, "debriefings" of survivors, and every type of counseling possible is being offered to the community, our churches and schools, businesses in lower Manhattan, pastors and teachers and care givers. FAITHFUL RESPONSE was formed to provide counseling and post trauma ministry in Long Island, especially with fire and rescue workers living there.

New Ground is a day camp for New York neighborhoods sponsored by LDRNY in partnership with Camp Koinonia, Lutheran Counseling Center (and other social ministry organizations), and local Lutheran congregations and schools. In the first year New Ground provided one hundred one-week camps for two thousand children. The summer program continues to provide an atmosphere where feelings can be shared, grief counseling and healing are available, and the local parish or school can be connected to the ongoing needs of the neighborhood. This program hosts young people from across the country who come to New York for "servant ministry" projects. The offices of LDRNY overlook Ground Zero. NEW GROUND conducts "faith walks" at the site, ending at St. Paul's chapel for a time of reflection. I have hosted groups from many places in New York. I can be loquacious in describing the ministry in our synod, the disaster relief programs, life in the city. But I cannot speak at Ground Zero. I am grateful to the New Ground ministry and the faith walks. I listen, prayerfully served by this spiritual accompaniment.

Comfort and Renew is a grant program to encourage local parishes, schools, and community organizations of which Lutherans are a part, to devise programs to address the wave effects of the disaster. Grants of up to $15,000 were made available through the synod, and staff work with local parishes and schools to focus opportunities for ministry.

Respite care for pastors, teachers, and other caregivers is an ongoing ministry of the synod and district. Volunteer pastors from around the country were organized to provide relief for pastors who take a week (funded) of respite absence.

Lutheran Schools and Early Childhood Centers have been the focus for intense ministries since the early days of the disaster. Forty-seven children in our schools lost a parent.

Interfaith/Governmental Agencies LDR has been intimately involved from the beginning in collaborating, coordinating, leading the efforts of organizations like FEMA, Red Cross, OEM and others. Many meet in our synod offices. LDR has enabled the Lutheran community to be "pastor" to the many volunteers and agencies involved in this effort. The office of the bishop has been intimately involved in the many advocacy efforts to extend deadlines for relief, look out for the immigrant, and plan for rebuilding.

Synod and District Grants: Some LDRNY grants have been given to strengthen the office of bishop and synod for this ministry of being the church at Ground Zero. These grants have provided space and time for staff to coordinate the program of respite for pastors and caregivers, the parish grant process, support for ethnic and immigrant ministries made vulnerable after the attacks, and other staffing needs.

"Comfort, comfort, now my people, says your God. Speak tenderly to Jerusalem. . . . A voice cries out in the wilderness: 'Prepare the way of the Lord'" (Isaiah 40:1-3).

The comfort is specific, carnal, human.

⁂ The Orphan Grain Train rolled into the Bronx with a delivery of a semi-trailer of food to restock food pantries and soup kitchens in the five boroughs decimated by need since the attacks. Twenty local residents unloaded the food at St. Peter's Lutheran Church. Most are unemployed and LDRNY paid them a wage and gave them food coupons. (Children in shelters were up 29 percent the year after the attacks, with 31,064, the most since the depression).

⁂ Nancy, a first-grader at one of our Queens parish schools, lost her mother in the World Trade Center. She received a scholarship from LDRNY to cover her tuition. LDRNY has provided many scholarships.

⁂ Ken, a Queens father of two, lost not only his wife in the World Trade Center, but his apartment and belongings as well—devastated by smoke, dust, and debris. LDRNY gave him relocation assistance, help with his financial burden, and connections to other available help.

⁂ A female corrections officer lost her husband and was about to lose her house when she couldn't meet the mortgage payments. Project Life helped her coordinate assistance with the National Association of Realtors, which was helping out in such cases.

↝ John helped build one of the temporary morgues. After four months of living with death, John was having some trouble coping. LDRNY is providing one-on-one-counseling.

↝ Twenty-two of our pastors and lay leaders were trained and volunteered at Ground Zero. One volunteer wrote: "A firefighter was trying to be unemotional when he reported that they had hit a 'hot spot'—the bodies of eight firefighters had been recovered Thursday afternoon and Friday morning . . . perhaps the most poignant and sad was the construction worker curled up in a fetal position on a cot, totally inaccessible to any human touch, clutching a stuffed animal and a photo of his sister. She had been a hostess at Windows on the World. Her body has not been found. Her brother, the back hoe operator, keeps looking for her. As I passed by I saw that he was quietly sobbing."

↝ Pastor Joanne Bond and the members of Cross of Christ in Babylon, Long Island, prepared and published an Epiphany devotional written by members and friends of the synod reflecting on their experience of the tragedy. Many were at Ground Zero or in ministry with those who lost loved ones. They made a copy available to every member of our synod. Joanne's devotion makes this event accessible to all of us, not only in New York but everywhere: "For New Yorkers, it doesn't matter if you didn't lose a relative or friend in the attacks. We feel like we were all attacked. Each day, when we read in the *New York Times* about the many people who lost their lives in this senseless tragedy, we feel like we knew them. They were people like us . . . many so young, people who worked, people who loved . . . special people."

These and other programs continue. As needs or intensity changes, support shifts to where it is needed most. LDRNY will not "move on" as long as this tragedy lasts. We are the last faith-based group still doing case management. The association of victim's family members has its offices in the LDRNY

"Comfort and Renew" suite of offices downtown. Ours will be the last dollar spent. "You shall be called the repairer of the breach, the restorer of streets to live in" (Isaiah 58:12).

Magnificat

My father was a church organist and choir director. When I was very small my parents bought their first record player and two records: Bach's *Magnificat* and Rogers and Hammerstein's *South Pacific*. They tell me that I listened to these records all the time. This was when I was just learning to speak a few words. My father says I bounded through the house singing the "Fecit Potentiam" chorus from the *Magnificat* in Latin ("He has shown strength with his arm and scattered the proud . . .). Or all of a sudden burst out, "ain't that too damn bad!" from *South Pacific*.

It seems right to mate Mary's song with Broadway show tunes in the imagination and sensory world of a child. I didn't understand the words, but the music moved me to speech and song, as it still does. From ecstatic spiritual speech, "magnificat," to carnal affirmation: "there is nothing like a dame. . . ." The holy is here, in this world. From an audience with an angel Mary proceeds, pregnant, to the kitchen table of her cousin Elizabeth. Her reaction to the Gospel promise, received in ecstatic vision from an angel and physically present in her belly, is similar to that of the shepherds and all disciples who heard angelic good news. She goes in haste to share it. Like a child who does not know fully the meaning of the words yet is moved to join the melody, Mary sings along with the holy all around her. Her cousin Elizabeth blesses Mary, for her womb and for her faith: "Blessed is the fruit of your womb. . . . And blessed is she who believed that there would be a fulfillment of what was spoken to her by the Lord" (Luke 1:42, 45).

Mary, in turn, blesses God. She translates the Gospel into what it means for everyday people: the hungry, the empty, the poor. She moves from angel's song to show tunes as she translates religion into life, tradition into hope. She mixes creed, "the promise he made to our ancestors, to Abraham," with human society, "from generation to generation" (Luke 1:55, 50). Her song is countercultural: the proud are scattered, the powerful brought down, the lowly lifted up, the hungry filled, the rich sent empty away. That is the arc of hope and promise in every tragedy.

Mary's Magnificat includes us here in New York this fifth anniversary since the September 11 attacks left our skyline bereft of its downtown mooring. The Magnificat includes the Ground Zeros of every community and every human life. Like a child hearing and repeating the beautiful tunes and text, we don't always comprehend the meaning of it all. But the Magnificat washes over us. From the sixteenth-story offices of Lutheran Disaster Response, we and our many interfaith partners look directly into the pit where the towers came down. I remember an Advent open house for this new space for healing and grace. Along the fence around the site you can see pictures of a street exhibit of the history of the towers, along with messages and remembrances. The familiar vertigo takes over and one is immediately back on that terrible day. The busy construction seems a lie covering the chaos of that day which is still loose in the city. I move from the window and look into the next office. Clustered together are a group of families of the victims. This is their space too. Here they are welcome, here they pray, plan, meet counselors, advocate for use of the pit below us as holy ground, a place for remembrance as well as resurgent commerce. A man whose brother rests in the rubble sixteen stories down speaks of how this holy season is both the hardest time, and also a time of hope and faith. "My soul magnifies the Lord, and my spirit rejoices in God my Savior, for he has looked with favor on the lowliness of his servant" (Luke 1:47).

We were in a Chinatown restaurant to mark the one-year anniversary of "New Life," an LDRNY program aimed at Chinese Fujianese immigrants, those at the bottom in our city. On that awful day in September hard lives became nearly impossible.

Thousands of jobs were lost. Those without documents were also without work, health care, and often housing. We heard ten Fujianese children tell their stories, remarkable acts of public courage given their cultural instinct for silence about anything personal. They told of growing up without their fathers who had come to this country years ago to secure a new life for the rest of the family. They described awkward and joyful reunions in New York. "Surely, from now on all generations will call me blessed. . . . His mercy is for those who fear him from generation to generation" (Luke 1:48).

They spoke of beatings in school, sick parents, homelessness, gangs and drugs and fear, domestic violence, desperate searches for work. Decaying public schools and inaccessible health care is the reality in immigrant communities in this city. And after 9/11 what remained of any safety net came completely apart. New Life has been a lifeline, they told us. These young people are learning English, were able to spend a week at a local Lutheran college, were fighting for hope and a future. Some of their friends had committed suicide. They sang us a song which sounded like the Magnificat, the Lou Rawls hymn to human solidarity, "Lean on me." "He has . . . lifted up the lowly; he has filled the hungry with good things" (Luke 1:52, 53).

One of the case managers for Project Life, a program of Lutheran Social Services and LDRNY, was at the end of his hope. He had been working with a Dominican immigrant with three young children who lost her housekeeping job when the Marriott downtown was destroyed. It was at a time when all the emergency housing and other programs came to an end. She went back to her husband who had been beating her. He threw her and the children out. The case manager, a young college graduate in his first job, took her desperate situation into his own heart. One thing after another fell through. "My back is against the wall," he sobbed to his supervisor. Mary sings for him, and for the mother and her babies who inhabit his tears. Sometimes the song sounds more like hope than reality: "He has scattered the proud in the thoughts of their hearts. He has brought down the powerful from their thrones, and lifted up the lowly" (Luke 1:51, 52).

One Sunday I preached at one of our congregations in the South Bronx. The assisting minister is the fiancé of one of the deacons of our synod, who is serving a life term in prison. He has organized a congregation behind walls with the young men who are at risk in prison, with Bible studies, support groups, prayer groups, and worship. A choir of children sang a beautiful Gospel song. In this poorest congressional district in America the church was filled with faith and hope. As they came for communion, many stopped by the prayer deacons and pastor for anointing and prayer for healing. An acolyte with a towel wiped the tears and sweat from the pastor pleading with God for the healing of his flock. This parish lost several loved ones and many jobs on September 11. During the sermon I took a rock from my pocket. "This rock is from Ground Zero. A firefighter who rescued many on September 11 and who survived gave it to me. He noticed that I had trouble getting through a sermon several weeks after the disaster. He waited for me in the narthex and gave me this. He told me: 'Every time you feel this rock remember that Jesus, the rock of our salvation, was downtown that day and is with you always.'" Mary and her song take so many forms in the city. "He has helped his servant Israel, in remembrance of his mercy, according to the promise he made to our ancestors, to Abraham and to his descendants forever" (Luke 1:54, 55).

We hear Mary's song in the midst of life's tragedies. We sing it with those around the world—the Red River Valley, Oklahoma City, Darfur, Beirut, Haifa, Madrid, London, New Orleans, Banda Aceh. In Mary's song we hear the angel's promise of incarnation. God with us: the repairer of the breach. Like a dazzled child we may not fully understand it. But its sound is beautiful and we come with haste to join the song. Magnificat.

5. Compassionate Vocation

"Then the Lord said, 'I have observed the misery of my people who are in Egypt; I have heard their cry on account of their task-masters. Indeed, I know their sufferings, and I have come down to deliver them.' . . . But Moses said to God, 'If I come to the Israelites and say to them, "The God of your ancestors has sent me to you," and they ask me, "What is his name?" what shall I say to them?' God said to Moses 'I AM WHO I AM.'"

—Exodus 3:7, 13, 14

In the Wilderness

"What do you see now?" he asked. "Don't think, don't question, just be present to the images. Follow your senses. What do you see now?" We are about an hour into a session of EMDR trauma counseling. This is a process that stimulates right and left brain responses using sound, eye movement, and other stimuli as a way of addressing traumatic experiences and reliving them in a healing way. It seems a little "out there" to me. But it is eight months since September 11, and I have been carrying around a load of hurt, I have been encouraging other pastors and caregivers to get help and now it's time for me. The doctor has pioneered this process and trained many, including some of our counselors. He and his colleagues have been in the fire houses, with survivors and bereaved loved ones. After half an hour of conversation I am urged to go back in my mind to my office window on September 11, to Ground Zero several days later.

Here is what I see from the sixteenth-floor window of the Interchurch Center, with an unobstructed view south: A smoky collar around Tower One in the brilliant fall sunshine and blue. Aimless thoughts about "Jersey dirty socks air" poaching the pristine lower Manhattan skyline. The stricken face of my executive assistant, her shrill, strained voice: "This is terrible, turn on your radio!" Her face. Her face. The towers, our backyard, disappearing in a smoky haze. Sounds of the sea pass from left to right through earphones. Eyes clenched tight. Her face. The smoky blur out the window. The gnaw in the gut which I have been carrying for eight months, helpless fear.

I see nothing at Ground Zero. Nothing. "Where are you most tense in your body?" A line across the bridge of my nose is tight, shooting pain. "Stay there. Just stay with the tension." I am breathing through my nose, my lower face covered with a mask. I am at Ground Zero and afraid to smell death. It comes through intermittently and I choke on the sweet fragrance, then labor with renewed diligence and concentration to breathe through my mouth. Then I see the ground. The feet covered with boots. The rubble, shards of glass. The scream of engines and machines. I look up and am shocked at the immensity of the carnage. I can't move, look down, and follow feet. Soon memory gives the images back to me. Hard and stricken faces approaching me and nodding, muttering "thank you," asking for a prayer, sharing something hard and sad, again and again, "Pray for me, Father." I had forgotten the smell until it came back, releasing my sinuses from eight months of pressure. We get through it. I am crying.

We have been to the window and breathed at Ground Zero. A cleansing, albeit ephemeral. The doctor has me relax into my body again, paying attention to what I am feeling and seeing, meant, I think, to yield a final healing or hopeful image. "What do you see now?" What I see is so clear it takes my breath away.

I sit at a desk of a retreat house in the Arizona desert in January of 2000. A picture of something holy, an icon or something is on the wall. I have just spoken to my urologist whose phone call found me in the desert. He has told me that I have prostate cancer and there is a sense of urgency in his voice. "Call me as soon as you get back to town."

The therapist tells me that sometimes when we begin to deal with the immediate trauma other memories take a number, wait for a hearing. Guess you still have some work to do with that one, he said. I am back there, about to pick up the phone again. "Honey, it's me. I talked to the urologist." That's as far as I got.

So this is something I bring to the flame which burns and consumes.

A tragedy is like a refiner's fire. It burns, destroys, yet also purifies. In hundreds of spiritual conversations with people inside and outside of the church I have come to believe that a great communal tragedy like September 11 brings people to a burning bush of sorts. Vocation comes into view as well as the road we have traveled to get to this moment. Who are we? Where have we been? How can we live lives that matter? Our healing comes from the experiences and biographies which came before it. If prayer has been hardwired into us by nature (image of God) and nurture (grandmother's bedtime rituals), then these things break forth from us and become gifts God uses for comfort, renewal, and healing. God prepares us, institutionally and individually, for those moments when God will work through us in times of tragedy.

The story of Moses and the burning bush is an outstanding example of biography meeting vocation. The one who calls is moved by compassion: "For I have seen the suffering of my people . . ." Through the gifts and life experiences of pastors, lay leaders, and institutions, grace was all around us, reminding us that we were baptized for this moment.

Curiosity in the Desert

What was it about the burning bush and this call to ministry in the breach which made the Moses story so compelling over the centuries? This call does not come in a religious place—from the mountaintop, the temple, the church. It comes in the desert, a non-religious, God-forsaken place. The call finds us where we are. Today's wilderness looks like this: a time of financial and spiritual pressure on the church; a time of war and tragedy; a time when the stranger among us is not welcome; a time when it seems that mainline Protestantism is heading into a perfect storm and its very survival in this post-modern culture is up for grabs; a time when ministries feel "at risk." The wilderness is when tragedy strikes, when our relationships crumble, when a loved one dies, when the towers fall, the hurricane rips, the diagnosis comes. In the wilderness the bush appears, the call comes with no display of divine power. God piques Moses' curiosity and draws him to the bush. A questing, curious spirituality leads to the call.

Seneh, The Fire That Doesn't Burn

In Exodus 3:2, the Hebrew word for "bush" is *seneh,* a word which appears only here and in Deuteronomy 33:16 ("the Presence in the bush"). Perhaps this is a word play on "Sinai," pointing toward the revelation on the mountain later in the Exodus narrative. A burning bush not consumed caught Moses' attention. We have too many recent images of flames which burn and consume—the holocaust, suicide bombs in Iraq, towers turning to fiery furnaces, and church fights which threaten to burn a hole right through us. Fires of conflict consume some of our relationships. Fires rage in the breach of our cities, suburbs, and towns: teen violence, poverty, abuse, aids, homelessness, hunger, wars. The blazing fire of unbelief in our society which cannot tell the old, old story of Jesus and does not know how to call on the Name of the Lord. Moses is confronted with another kind of fire: a fire of God that burns without consuming, a holy flame in the wilderness that will not be quenched. This is the fire Jesus longed to see in lukewarm believers: "I wish you were either hot or cold" (Revelation 3:15). This is the fire Jeremiah was weary of holding in and which erupted from him in fiery prophesy. This fire of God meets the consuming fire of tragedy.

Who Is Moses? Who Are You?

Why is God attracted to Moses? Moses is a murderer. He has commitments and gifts. He brings to the *seneh* three interventions against instances of injustice: when a slave was mistreated; when he "looked this way and that" and killed the Egyptian brutalizing his kinsman; with a woman at a well. God saw that Moses would not tolerate the strong abusing the weak. Moses has these gifts in part because of his Egyptian upbringing. He owes his life to a conspiracy of Hebrew and Egyptian women, solidarity of the poor and privileged. They heard the vulnerable Moses cry, were moved to compassion, and acted to save the baby. God in Exodus will mirror their actions. God affirms the many gifts and experiences etched into the soul and character of Moses before the encounter in the wilderness.

Who are you? What are your life experiences and gifts? God is interested in biography, in the sum of who you are and what you bring to the table. How has God been preparing you for the burning bush and for vocation at the fires of tragedy?

What We Bring to the Fire

We had experienced disaster response before the towers fell. In what vulnerable places have you experienced grace? At first I wanted to hide after the diagnosis. But being a bishop isn't a recipe for privacy. Two previous bishops had cancer and one had died. There were rumors starting already. I decided to do what I had asked, as a parish pastor, of the members of the congregations I served: reach out for help; it's all right to be vulnerable. After a pastoral letter to our membership sharing basic facts, I was scheduled to lead worship the next four Sundays in churches in our synod before the surgery. It was one of the most spiritual experiences of my life. There was the extended time of prayer at the storefront church in the Bronx. There was the children's lesson in Long Island in which I was asked to be Peter's mother-in-law (the Gospel text for the day). I sat in a chair in the chancel. The pastor began to tell the story of the healing of Peter's mother-in-law. "What do we do when someone like Peter's mother-in-law is sick?" "We write cards," and so children filed to the front and gave me cards they had made for Peter's mother-in-law. "What else do we do when someone like Peter's mother-in-law is sick?" "We pray for them!" And so little hands stretched out to my head. "Oh, Lord, listen to your children praying," they sang and prayed for Peter's mother-in-law. It was a time of wondrous communal pastoral care. Congregations sent Sunday bulletins with my name highlighted in magic marker in the endless list of names on the parish prayer list. Those who had faced this cancer reached out and helped me name and tame the unknown which terrified me.

A peace descended. A couple of days before the surgery my wife and I were listening to Bach's "Mass in B" at Carnegie Hall. I thought: how unlikely to receive the gift of life in the first place. How astonishing this life has been, work worth doing, people who love me. It was with a sense of gratitude that I faced the surgery.

I was interviewed for *More Magazine* (a supplement to *Good Housekeeping*) in an article with other prostate cancer survivors including Joe Torre and Harry Belafonte. My words about the spiritual dimensions of this experience were edited out of the final draft. They were more interested in the prurient than the sacred, in biological details (which I discussed frankly) than the spiritual ones. With my faith edited out of the narrative, I asked them to take my story out of their article. This struck a chord in the interviewer. We talked about tragedy and faith. She restored the spiritual journey to the article. When tragedy strikes, we bring our souls to the party.

I brought three phrases from this experience to the burning bush and burning buildings.

I'll Pray for You

No more a pious bromide but a sustaining power. All the prayers kept me in the hands of my Creator and the peace of the Healer. All those times I had said, "I'll pray for you," and meant it and did it in a kind of Protestant work ethic drill. Never again, I say. Those are holy words. To pray for someone is a bit like creation. The person appears before you in all her or his particularity and originality. To pray for someone shrinks the distance between the one who prays and the one in the heart of the prayer, mirroring the ministry of Jesus whose cross and resurrection closes the distance between God and you and me.

Pastor's Here

Lying on the gurney in the hallway outside the door that says, "Keep Out," waiting for the surgery, I was filled with anxiety. Then my wife said these words of comfort: "Stephen, pastor's here." Pastor's here. My pastor stood over me, not just a nice guy, but a representative of the community of Jesus, a reference point to God's promises, a reminder that I am not the first one ever to have to trust God into the unknown. We prayed the Lord's Prayer. He blessed me, tracing the sign of the cross on my forehead. Re-enchantment, if you will, as they pushed me through the doors. Later, during a time of depression while at home recovering, my dear friend and bishop from Ohio got on a plane in Cleveland and flew to New York. When he showed up with bread and wine I began to move from the cave into the sunlight. Pastor's here.

Soup's On

When I was brought home to recover, hot meals began appearing at our front door. Without any fuss the members of our congregation fed us every day for two weeks. We were connected to hope and to community by these elemental acts of kindness. The title of my favorite Raymond Carver short story is "A Small, Good Thing." The title refers to freshly baked bread and, indeed, the small, good thing of food at our doorstep was manna on our road to healing.

I'll pray for you. Pastor's here. Soup's on. I learned to trust the power of these small, good things. Prayer, pastoral presence, small acts of kindness became the foundation of disaster response. And I already knew their power in a time of seeming powerlessness.

Collective Biography

We bring our institutional biographies as well as our personal ones to the burning bush of God's calling and consuming flames of tragedy. One of the biggest issues to emerge from the 9/11 attacks is how we treat the stranger among us. Immigrants, economic migrants, refugees, asylum seekers are a meta-issue today. What kind of a society will emerge from Ground Zero? What kind of a people will we become? In a synod that worships in twenty-five languages these issues were with us before the attacks. One immigrant I had met about a year before the attacks was close to my heart in the days after the attacks as we tried to bring relief and comfort to many strangers. Her name is Lisa K. and she is a fifteen-year-old child of God from Congo. I met her during a tour of the INS detention center near Kennedy Airport with other New York religious and political leaders. The tour had been set up by Lutheran Immigration and Refugee Services to shed light on how refugees, including children, are treated when they come to America. Basically, we put them in jail.

Lisa fled Congo when her family was taken away by government troops for supporting deposed President Mobutu. They are presumed dead. Her mother had gone ahead to Canada to seek asylum. Lisa was on her way to meet her. At JFK airport to transfer planes she was questioned by INS officials and given a dental test on which basis they claimed her to be an adult. They put an orange jumpsuit on her and threw her into the detention center. Our visit with her was painful. It was conducted in Lingala through an interpreter. She was very depressed, had no one with whom she could speak, and had lost weight because she had been unable to eat regularly. It was obvious she was a scared child. She stared at the floor and kept a finger in her mouth as she hid her face from us. I asked her if anyone had offered her spiritual counsel or the opportunity to pray. I folded my hands as she looked at me and began to tear up. She is a Christian, she said through the interpreter. No one had offered her spiritual comfort. She shook her head and looked back at the floor. It is hard enough being a fifteen-year-old girl under normal circumstances. She spends twenty-three hours a day locked up with no windows. She had been there four months.

The tour ended with "grip and grin" photo opportunities and interviews with religious and political leaders. Then everyone went home. We came back. Our synod's East African ministry joined me in giving personal and sustained attention to Lisa. We advocated on behalf of asylum seekers and asked for Lisa's release to join her mother in Canada. The pastor and members of the Swahili- and Lingala-speaking Lutheran community visited Lisa every day. They prayed, comforted, and shared spiritual nurture and hope with Lisa. With every visit the light of truth and justice broke into this insulting place and kept the pressure of God's grace in the breach. This ministry accompanied Lisa to her hearings, interceded on her behalf, and sponsored her during the asylum-seeking process. Finally they let her go. We brought this piece of our collective biography to the refiner's fire on September 11.

Not Ready for Prime Time

God brought the collective biography of the children of Israel to the burning bush. Moses brought his own biography. Like a second career candidate for ministry, Moses turned his face from this fire, "for he was afraid to look at God" and makes eight objections. What if they don't believe my story about a burning bush? I don't talk so good. Send someone else. The candidacy process has begun. Why did Moses hide his face? I think it was because God was confronting Moses with the pain of his people. It was too hard to see. He had to look away. "I have seen the suffering of my people."

God called from the breach and Moses didn't want to see it. When the Jewish people were suffering terribly in the land of Egypt, God was with them in their pain. Moses is not alone in turning his face from the God in the breach. Much of the suffering in today's world is a result of the deeds, misdeeds, and non-deeds of those who live only for themselves, who turn away from Darfur, the poor, the stranger, the vulnerable. In *Letters and Papers from Prison* (New York: Macmillan 1953), Dietrich Bonhoeffer criticized the church from a prison cell: "Our church has been fighting in these years only for its self-preservation, as though that were an end in itself. Now it is incapable of taking the word of reconciliation and redemption to the world."

Discipleship and vocation begin here: how then shall we live? Will we face the *"seneh"* and see the God who is afflicted in the sufferings of his people?

The Call to Ministry Begins a Holy Conversation and God Is Ready with Plan B

In the midst of Moses' objections, God honors his side of the conversation. Moses' objections move from worshipful response to almost testy conversation. God draws him out and works with him. Trust that your restless spirit and the emotions of deep vocational decisions are the stuff of divine conversation and the Holy Spirit's discerning wisdom. Even though he stutters, is inarticulate, Moses holds his own in this conversation. Moses' questions and insights point to the task ahead with Pharaoh. God goes to Plan B. Aaron is dealt in. The God of history is known in deep relationship, in the struggle of contemplation. God is not the only one with something important to say. And isn't that the gift of prayer, that God truly wants to give us an ear? Our response to God's call can contribute to shaping the future; we are not just passive recipients. God works with our frailties, our doubts, as well as our strengths. God can work with a church like ours, with someone like you and me.

The Heart of All Ministry and Every Call: God Is Calling from the Breach

God's goal is not to make life more bearable in the breach of slavery in Egypt. God is about rescue. God sees and cries out with the pain of the people God loves: "I have seen the affliction of my people. . . . I know their suffering." God had entered the pain, a pain which is burning brightly in the *seneh* of tragedy. The cross is no stranger to this kind of God. Unlike Pharaoh, whose heart is hardened, God's heart melts in the fire which burns but does not consume. God is not rendered powerless in the breach, but finds a way to move into Israel's situation to deliver the people. That's why God calls to mission. This is the good news about which Mary would sing. God takes sides and calls to vocation to become God's partners in taking sides with the vulnerable and suffering. God will accompany the Word with actions and partners that make the Word work. That is why God is calling you and me God's body, the church on earth. When Moses was able to look into the bush, he became a co-participant with God in the rescue. In Exodus 14:31 we hear that the people "believed in the Lord and in his servant Moses." We hear echoes of Romans 10:14 as God keeps calling over these centuries: "How are they to believe in one of whom if they have never heard? And how are they to hear without someone to proclaim him?" Every vocation issues from the compassionate heart of God who sees the affliction of the people and is determined to act on their behalf. Every individual and collective biography points toward participation in this gracious deliverance.

Moses: "Who Am I?" and "Who Are You?" God: "I Am Who I Am." God Calls to True Identity

So Moses, and we, may initially hide our faces from God but God still calls from the breach in Exodus 3:9: "'The cry of the Israelites has now come to me; I have also seen how the Egyptians oppress them. So come, I will send you to Pharaoh to bring my people, the Israelites, out of Egypt.' But Moses said to God, 'Who am I that I should go to Pharaoh, and bring the Israelites out of Egypt?'" At the burning bush Moses says, "Here I am." Then God answers the question "Who am I?" and challenges Moses with "Who are you?" Moses, on the run from murder, confronts himself in the desert. Dennis Jacobsen, in his book on community organizing, writes: "Who, indeed is Moses? Slave or prince? Hebrew or Egyptian or Midianite? Murderer of shepherd? Fugitive or liberator?" (*Doing Justice* [Minneapolis: Fortress Press, 1987], 56). Unless Moses discovers who he really is, he is of little use to the freedom struggle of the Hebrew slaves. God challenges Moses to see himself in the way that God sees him: the bold liberator of the Hebrew people. In his encounter with God's call to compassion and liberation Moses now knows who he is.

God challenges us to see ourselves—individually and collectively as the church—as God sees us: not cringing refugees from post-Constantine Christendom, but a movement to reconcile the world in the shadow of the cross; not broken refugees from tragedy, but wounded healers. God's disaster response is the church and its narrative of the death and resurrection of Jesus, acted out in numerous ways. Pastor's here. I'll pray for you. Soup's on. Repairers of the breach.

The struggle of Moses for his identity at the burning bush causes God to give Moses God's name and identity: "I am who I am." "I'll be there for you." The giving of the name is as important as the meaning of the name. God offers a relationship, closeness, communication. The God in the breach, in the fire that does not consume is *Abba*.

Who are we together as the church or individually as spiritual seekers? This struggle for identity is a spiritual struggle. As one comes to know the God in the breach, one comes to know oneself. Becoming oneself is not a solitary trek, and that goes against the grain of our age. Rabbi Hillel suggested that when Moses "looked this way and that and saw no man and then slew the Egyptian," he wasn't looking to see that the coast was clear. He was looking for help. And that God's call to liberation, the whole Exodus narrative, was about Moses never again being in the position of "looking this way and that and seeing no man." It is about the creation of community. Moses cannot discover his true self in isolation. The God in the breach and the bush called him to his people. God's disaster response is community.

Who will we become as servants of the church—as pastors, lay leaders, spiritual people? Ministry among people in the breach can reveal to us our lost identity and save the soul of a church that often lives like a stranger to its calling and its God. The Great Commission and the Great Commandment will be the refining fire of our true identity.

Every tragedy calls us to the communal journey to compassionate vocation and the freedom to serve God and all humanity. It is the collective walk to which God calls us. "You shall be called repairers of the breach, restorers of streets to live in." And God still gives us the divine name. "Go therefore and make disciples of all nations, baptizing them in the name of the Father and of the Son and of the Holy Spirit, and teaching them to obey all that I have commanded you. And remember, I am with you always, to the end of the age" (Matthew 28:19, 20).

Moses learned such truths in his journey to the breach, to justice, a vocation as a light to the nations. It started at the burning bush, offering light in the breach of God's afflicted people. May it ignite our life together after every tragedy.

The Next Burning Bush

God is always leading us to the fire of compassion that is at the heart of all vocation. A burning bush in my first parish ministry transformed the way I regard my vocation and that of the church. On the night of my installation as pastor of Atonement Lutheran Church in Jackson Heights, Queens, New York, the stones starting flying and most of the stained glass windows were shattered. Vandalism continued as I began ministry with a "congregation at risk" in a neighborhood undergoing massive ethnic and economic change. The neighborhood teemed with vulnerable children, many of them from poor and immigrant homes. The church averted its eyes from the community. Its doors were locked and a fence protected the parking lot and play space. About thirty people came to worship in this fearful enclave on a Sunday. The congregation was struggling to find vision for the future. Then, almost too literally came the burning bush.

On the afternoon of Christmas Eve two boys started a fire at the church door. They took a swing at the secretary as she tried to stop them. I grabbed both of the young boys, dragged them to the altar, and talked to them about the crèche, the animals, and the people around the manger. We walked around the repaired and cracked stained glass windows, each depicting events in the life of Jesus. "Ask questions," I said. They did. They were immigrants from Nicaragua, living with an uncle. I called the uncle and told him what happened and that I would be having supper with the boys. I invited them to come back for the Christmas Eve service. One did. He eventually became an acolyte in our church. But in that sanctuary my vocation began to take shape. In telling the story of Christmas, of God coming to be with us, in willing the story into the ears and minds of these children of God, the story again became my own. God was calling with the voice of these children: "I have seen the affliction of my people . . . " We didn't avert our eyes and God opened our doors, our windows, the gates of our fences. Our congregation began a renewal of its journey to freedom and service. Tragedy is the fire lit at the entrance of our churches and our hearts, inviting the retelling of the story, acting with the compassion of the God in the breach.

6. Visitation

"In those days Mary set out and went with haste to a Judean town in the hill country, where she entered the house of Zechariah and greeted Elizabeth. When Elizabeth heard Mary's greeting, the child leaped in her womb. And Elizabeth was filled with the Holy Spirit and exclaimed with a loud cry, 'Blessed are you among women, and blessed is the fruit of your womb. And why has this happened to me, that the mother of my Lord comes to me? For as soon as I heard the sound of your greeting, the child in my womb leaped for joy. And blessed is she who believed that there would be a fulfillment of what was spoken to her by the Lord.' And Mary said, 'My soul magnifies the Lord, and my spirit rejoices in God my Savior.'"

—Luke 1:39-46

Hic

"In the sixth month the angel Gabriel was sent by God to a town in Galilee."

—Luke 1:26

The first visitation was from an angel. *Verbum Carnem Factum Est*. The Word became flesh. I saw those Latin words carved into an altar in a crypt chapel at the Church of the Annunciation in Nazareth, the place where Mary heard the news that she was in the family way. I noticed one other little word that could only be written in that place and it almost gave me a heart attack. *Verbum Carnem Hic Factum Est. Hic. Here. Thus*. The Word was made flesh *here*! I thought about that. The divine explosion of love and grace and compassion from the heart of a gracious God came, "hic," "here," in the belly of this woman, Mary, in this struggling Arab town, in this world. God made flesh here. Hic. The visitation in her womb is a divine intrusion. When we receive or make a visit, we have to adjust, give space. Behind every visitation is the divine visitation of *verbum carnem factum est* . . . hic, right here . . . rearranging our priorities, quickening our hope, disrupting our patterns, deepening our compassion. In our visits every place is a holy land. God is near.

Tragedy isolates. Visitation brings into propinquity the "hicness" of God. Communal responses are crucial to tragedy and disaster. Lamentations, post-trauma work, corporate prayer and liturgy, programs of comfort and renewal can only be done in relationships. We can claim our vocations only in relationship to our communities of faith. My colleagues who are bishops serving in the territory of Hurricane Katrina each described the power of visitation as the first steps toward coping, hoping, and making a stand. One, a volunteer rescue squad member for years, went right to the afflicted areas and worked along with the rescue workers. There was public silence from his office until he emerged and shared stories of devastation and faith, as seen from the ground. His colleague soon gathered New Orleans area Lutherans for a liturgy. Many had lost their churches. The visitation of this liturgy with their bishop was crucial for the stricken community of faith, as they found consolation in one another, carved out space for lamentations, shared their resources, and organized for servant ministry beyond themselves to the entire metropolis.

The presence of hope in the world, the comfort of the nearness of loved ones, the announcement of good news can only begin for us as it did for Mary. She received a visit, and then she made a visit. In the visit God comes near. Hic.

On the Road

"In those days Mary set out and went with haste . . . "
—Luke 1:39

Every journey worth taking begins in the heart, then the feet begin to move down the road. Mary's heart was so full with the angelic announcement that she had to be with kin. She set out on the road "with haste," an urgency later picked up by the shepherds who, also filled by an angelic announcement, "came with haste to find Mary and Joseph and the babe, lying in a manger." The little detail that she went to "a Judean town in the hill country" is worth repeating. The road was arduous and long for a newly pregnant woman on the road to connect with kin.

Sunday morning I accompanied the Tanzanian bishop to Bushasha, one of the most remote parishes in our companion diocese in Africa. We made a grueling journey over a road pitted by floods, worn away by the sun. I came with haste and full heart because this is the church building, bombed by Idi Amin and destroyed, where the people had been worshiping under a tree when I met them three years ago. Our synod had rebuilt the church and we were on our way to rededicate it. We knew that at some point the road would end and we would have to take a long walk on a small path to get to the church. The path had been widened, a celebratory arch of papyrus marked the beginning of a new road they had cut to meet us. They had "come with haste" to join us on the road. Singing children and drumming led the way along this new road until we arrived to dedicate the church—and I was privileged to baptize twenty-five children of God.

The day the work at Ground Zero officially came to an end was a hard day for those who had been giving their lives as volunteers and workers every day for many months. It was a sad day for those for whom Ground Zero became a final resting place for loved ones. On September 11 many people, with hearts breaking, "set out and went with haste" to and from Ground Zero on pathways of compassion, agony, heroism, comfort, and renewal. Those who had escaped were part of the visitation to our Manhattan, Brooklyn, and Bronx parishes. Along the road of soot and tears they were met with open doors and hearts. Visitation happened in local parishes and wider communities as we prayed and lit candles. We found roads to one another as kin in comfort and renewal. Police, fire, and emergency services vehicles "set out and went with haste" from Long Island, upstate New York, New Jersey, and later from all over the nation, to rescue and save. Over the next months Ground Zero, St. Paul's chapel, and the landfill sites in Staten Island became communities of extended visitation as search and rescue became recovery of the dead and we joined together as kin to comfort and renew.

In the weeks after September 11 my heart was moved and I "set out and went with haste" to listen to the stories of our pastors and people. I heard about visitations, public liturgies, acts of love and compassion. I knew in my heart that our pastors and people were also "in the breach," vulnerable and hurting in the midst of heroic ministry to a metropolis "in the breach." Visitations take so many forms.

Nine Months and Eight Hundred Miles Away

"My name is Nate and I will be confirmed next week. I was right in the middle of my two years of confirmation when tragedy struck your city. This letter is just to let you know that nine months and eight hundred miles away we still think about you and your losses . . . stay strong, Nate."

That was one of over thirty letters from a confirmation class of a congregation in Illinois, sent to our congregation in which the New York City fire commissioner is a member. Thousands of such letters came to our synod office, our congregations, our members.

From Leah: "I hope your grief is relieved little by little every day. We at my church pray for you often and feel sorry for your losses. We also want very much to understand your pain."

From Farrell: "In some way everyone has been affected by 9/11. I was affected. My father is an airline pilot for American Airlines and was flying on that day. Even though many lives were cut short, you must remember they are in a better place. 'Jesus, remember me when you come into your kingdom.' Even though it may seem like you are alone with your grief and hurt, you are not. God is always with you . . . and we wish to understand the pain you and many other people are going through. Have hope!"

A stuffed animal, posters, pictures, money from bake sales and Sunday school offerings. The visitation was immense. The lament—"Is it nothing to all you who pass by?"—was still being answered nine months and eight hundred miles away. In the visitation we knew that grace was all around us.

A Poem and an Open Door

A young man in New York City was living alone. His family is his congregation. At a recent memorial service for one of their members, he recalled September 11. He had been downtown and made his way back uptown to his apartment. He was lonely, afraid, at emotional loose ends. He traveled to the apartment of the person being remembered at the liturgy. He spoke of the comfort Marjorie Lorenz had given him. That visitation was life-giving for him. Think of all the visitations around the world in the wake of every tragedy when hearts and homes are opened up as channels for grace. The visitation took artistic form. Hymns, poems, pictures were forms the visitation took. A poem written by Marjorie Lorenz was read at the memorial, a poem which points us toward one another and the "hicness" of God after tragedy.

"Wind and sky with one intent, implacably somber.

The air, heavy with sorrow, unable to weep, weighs us down.

Have our hearts become sodden graves, unquiet with festering sorrow?

But disaster bequeathed us the living, each person you see,

The soul's body armor in shreds, the awful secret revealed

That flesh seeds only on the moment granted,

That we dance on trap doors.

The living are suddenly ours to see for the first time,

To study in tender discovery, adorning the Earth,

Glowing like coins of gold sifted through the fingers of God.

Our charges, our ward, our gifts.

They are ours, we are theirs. These are the terms of the will."

(*Afterwards: September 2001* by Marjorie Lorenz)

A Tale of Two Fire Engines

On September 11, ten firefighters lost their lives out of Ladder Co. 9 in the East Village. During recovery efforts the badly burned truck was pulled from the rubble covered with dust and debris and sent to the Seagrave Fire Apparatus Company factory in Richmond, Virginia, which had made the truck years earlier. Sixteen employees spent the next several weeks bringing Ladder 9 back to life, cleaning it, placing it on a new chassis, doing extensive bodywork, and giving it a new paint job. The production manager said, "Rebuilding this truck was very important to all of us. We're all very proud that we could give back to the city. We put in extra time and that extra bit of quality." When the truck was resurrected workers from Virginia brought the ladder truck back to the firefighters at Ladder Co. 9. A fire truck became a vision of hope, a visitation, a sign of grace all around us.

Last year a small "local color" piece on the news caught my attention. New York firefighters were going to New Orleans. One of the trucks they were driving to the disaster is a truck donated by Louisiana which saw duty at Ground Zero. As we were days away from the fourth anniversary of the September 11, 2001, attacks we were inundated with pictures of unrelieved suffering from Hurricane Katrina. How much each of us desired to do something, anything, to alleviate the pain and suffering! There had been such heroic effort from around the country to be present, helpful, to touch and heal. We offer our prayers, and we mean it and do it. We feel we can't do enough—helpless, powerless, yet filled with such compassion and a physical need to make a difference. We are proud and glad to see local folks, including a red fire engine donated by the state of Louisiana, head off to that Ground Zero on the Gulf on our behalf.

This is how all of America felt and responded five years ago to us. This wave of compassion, energy, improvised response, and prayers, was directed at us. People promised prayer and meant it. People in our Lutheran community in America sent almost $15 million in the first ten days, resources still being used for comfort and renewal here in New York. At Ground Zero I met EMS workers, iron workers, fire and rescue personnel, chaplains from around the world. As we behold the massive response and outpouring of compassion in the wake of Katrina, it is fitting to remember with gratitude the solidarity of visitation. There are so many ways to "go with haste" on the visitation road.

When You Visit

Reach out immediately and tangibly. This is the "knocking on the door" that the member of the World Council of Churches delegation was talking about when he said that we begin to heal each time we answer the door and tell what happened. Phone calls, letters, e-mails, flowers, or other things we send as a way of sending ourselves should flow when tragedy strikes. We hang on to these concrete signs of solidarity.

Establish as soon as possible the appropriate channel for monetary gifts. Tragedy and disaster evoke visceral responses. We want to respond, but there are a lot of opportunists and bottom-feeders out there. In our world, Lutheran Disaster Response is the gold standard. For international disasters, it is Lutheran World Relief. Get the contact information in front of people immediately.

If possible, send money. In the immediate hours and days after a disaster, flexibility is everything. Money enables immediate and appropriate response. We live in a culture in which many people like to make a "designer response," to meet their own needs rather than the needs on the ground. Used clothing, truckloads of Bibles, stuffed animals have their place, but initially those responding need to get what they need when they need it, and that means send money. Send it to appropriate networks: to local expressions of the church, the offices of the local bishop\president\presbyter\etc. They will coordinate and match needs and resources. I have seen resources overflow (and even overburden) individual congregations good at telling their story, while anonymous congregations with great needs depend on the solidarity of the collective church body.

Make sure your personal visit is timely and appropriate. Stay away until needed or invited. Bishops in New Orleans and the Gulf Coast spoke of people who showed up with truckloads of stuff and wanted to be housed and fed, taxing an already strained infrastructure. People descended on our office in New York unloading all kinds of things and expecting hospitality and access to Ground Zero before we had even caught our breath. Sometimes folks who reached out became irritated if e-mails or phone messages went unanswered. Remember that when disaster or tragedy strikes people will be running hard. Every message brought hope. Later, when I had a chance, I answered every phone call and e-mail, and personally thanked everyone who sent anything.

If you have a skill or vocation that is relevant to first response then visit as soon as possible. Trained counselors, rescue workers, disaster response leaders, those experienced in "defusing" traumatic experiences of first responders, experienced disaster response experts, construction and iron workers (if relevant to rescue and recovery) and other needed responders are most welcome.

On the local level arrange for people to gather for prayer and spiritual comfort. Open up space for re-enchantment, for people to take their questions, doubt, sorrow, space for rekindling of hope and solidarity.

Be persistent. Check in regularly in the months and year ahead. If you keep visiting, if you don't "move on," the message is conveyed that God's presence and compassion will also not "move on" until healing begins.

At the right time, visit. After the initial energy (and even euphoria) of attending to a disaster or tragedy, then depression, spiritual enervation, and physical exhaustion set in. A timely visit can be occasion for renewal of spirit.

Don't forget care and respite for the caregivers. Offer vacation homes to pastors and chaplains and first responders. If you are a pastor, offer to use your vacation to visit and preach at a congregation in a disaster area.

Listen. Articulate your faith. When you visit by mail, e-mail, phone, or in person always ask, "How are you doing?" And listen. Repeated articulation of lament is the path to healing. Share your faith in a way that does not shut off expressions of doubt, anger, or sorrow. But share your faith and always place the hands of those affected by tragedy into the hands of the visitor of grace.

Low Sunday

At the October 2001 Conference of Bishops meeting in Chicago, people kept asking me what they could do to help. Sometimes when we feel most powerless, the only thing we have to offer is our company and ourselves. I blurted out, "What if the bishops and some pastors from every synod just came to be with us in New York?" What seemed a spontaneous idea was really the deepest heart's desire.

On April 6 over two hundred visitors from almost every synod of the ELCA (including thirty-two bishops) "set out and went with haste" to join their kin in New York for comfort and renewal. They represented a continual visitation of over $15 million of relief aid, personal visits, expressions of support, and a massive visitation of extended prayer. Their visitation was also an expression of thanks to the church in New York who had represented them as the Church at Ground Zero. On the Saturday after Easter we all came together for a liturgy at Madison Avenue Presbyterian Church attended by almost a thousand visitors and New Yorkers.

The next day, Easter 1, 2002 ("low Sunday"), these visitors fanned out to one hundred fifty of our congregations to preach and lead worship for us. The text of the sermons was the Gospel for Easter 1, the story of Doubting Thomas. These sermons were a chronicle of pastoral theology "on the run," dispatches of comfort from every area of the country delivered personally to our beleaguered metropolis. We collected them and published a book titled *The Cross at Ground Zero: Reflections and Sermons in Response to 9\11.*

In *The Plague* by Albert Camus, the doctor observes an old man looking into a window at his own reflection. Many people had died in the plague, including the old man's wife. The doctor reflects: "He knew what the old man was thinking as his tears flowed and thought it, too; that a loveless world is a dead world, and always there comes an hour when one is weary of prisons, of one's work and devotion to duty, and all one craves for is a loved face, the warmth and wonder of a human heart."

It was these "loved faces" we craved, the incarnate presence of the church. Hic. In the way of Jesus, propinquity is everything. In the presence of loved faces on "low Sunday," we looked up from the abyss and still believed that grace is all around us.

Each of these visitations has been a gracious expression of our kinship in Christ. Each visitation on parched and devastated roads has taken much effort. Behind the difficult journeys and the improvised roads has been the faith that this mutual connecting on the road is worth it, that the resolve to stay connected is somehow as central to our spiritual values and life of faith as that of a pregnant woman setting out through the hill country to her pregnant kin. "Mary entered the house of Zechariah and greeted Elizabeth. When Elizabeth heard Mary's greeting, the child leapt in her womb. And Elizabeth was filled with the Holy Spirit, and exclaimed with a loud cry, 'Blessed are you among women'" (Luke 1:41, 42).

Church as Visitation on the Road

"You shall be called repairer of the breach, restorer of roads to live in . . ."

Standing on the ridge of the mountain in Tanzania where the Ruhija Seminary African Arts and Music School is located, one can look into the valley below. One sees the smoke from cooking fires, the lush green of the banana and coffee shambas, clusters of huts, goats, and other signs of life lived pretty close to the bone. No electricity, running water, or major roads are in the near future in this valley. And one can see, crisscrossing the shambas, connecting the lone huts and village clusters, a network of paths cut into the dense foliage. These paths are life itself, in the same way that the paths up and down the stairways of the Twin Towers were matters of life and death and rescue.

Along these paths midwives travel to deliver babies, mourners travel with comfort for the bereaved, food travels to the market, the hungry and lonely are visited with bread and company, the isolated hut is connected to news and gossip, lovers meet, dusty young feet trudge to school, medicine is brought to the sick, the evangelist arrives at a hut to lead a village Bible study, the pastor brings the Eucharist to the aged and sick, help arrives to pick the harvest, the person dying of aids or malaria receives visitors who hold off the final loneliness. Up and down the paths of the towers rescue workers ascended and the rescued descended. One can see on the African and Manhattan pathways a pregnant woman going with haste to be with kin, kicking in her belly the promise that God inhabits the pathways, in life and death, comfort and renewal.

Standing on the ridge and seeing the roads and paths hacked out of the bush in this valley parish; standing at Ground Zero and seeing the incredible paths forged for rescue and recovery, comfort and renewal; standing in the narthex of Madison Avenue Presbyterian Church on "low Sunday" watching the long line of white-robed visitors from around the country in path of procession to the altar; standing in the new church of Bushasha at the end of a new road; pondering in my heart a vision of Mary who "set out and went with haste" to be with kin; all have given me vivid images of our life together as spiritual people, of the tidal wave of re-enchantment. *Religion* means literally to connect again: "re" means "again"; "ligione" (ligament) means "to connect." The word for synod is similar, literally "together on the road," ("*syn*" + "*hodos*"). Richard Lischer in *Open Secrets*, his beautiful book about a rural Lutheran parish, compares these rural roads to the connectedness and community of the perfect love of the Holy Trinity. "As the Father has loved me, so have I loved you" (John 15:9).

The fundamental fact of human existence is that we hunger all our lives for spiritual meaning, for a sense of the soul's destination, for connection with God and one another. Think of the human longing for companionship and holiness expressed in all these visions of roads and pathways. Can we see our families, friends, congregations, church bodies, and visitation after tragedy as a series of roads and pathways, connecting us to one another and the grace all around us? Hic. We are kin in Christ. "And Mary set out and went with haste." "You shall be called repairer of the breach, the restorer of roads to live in."

The Visit

The first visitation is from God. The angel appeared to Zechariah and Mary, announcing a visitation of babies as a sign of God's presence on the road. When the pregnant kin finally embrace, Elizabeth blesses Mary, and Mary blesses God. "My soul magnifies the Lord . . ." Magnificat.

Look who is present at the visitation. There is a mute priest and father, struck dumb by his narrow expectations of God, forced to be silent as new life begins to emerge in the bellies of his wife and her cousin. Let us be honest. Some of us have been struck mute, or something near it by the tragic events of 9/11, Katrina, personal tragedies and their aftermath among us. Some of us have seen our faith and zeal slowly erode and our expectations diminish. We have been giving and giving until we are empty. Sometimes even faith itself is elusive. We are numb with sorrow, or bereft of the right word at the right time. The world is telling us to "move on" and we may even tell ourselves to "get over it." But we can't. It gives me comfort that mute Zechariah is allowed to be present at the visitation, for we know that we will be there as well.

Even the Easter before "low Sunday" that year was low key, a sober but sure reflection on the resurrection of Jesus from the dead. We don't yet see the new life, the baby for which we hope. But dear friends, the pregnant mothers join us at this visitation, their unseen but kicking presence a sure sign of unseen nascent life among us. At this visitation Mary and Elizabeth join our own experience of mute and yet hopeful life for our ministries and ourselves. "The breach" in the walls of our metropolis has a place at the table through Mary's song: "He has lifted up the lowly; he has filled the hungry with good things." And Mary's song echoes the hope of Isaiah 58:11, 12: "You shall be like a watered garden. . . . Your ancient ruins shall be rebuilt."

For me, all the visitation roads meet at the table when the church gathers for Holy Communion. Mute, spiritually tired priests and baptized Christians, expectant believers, unseen kicking life in the wombs of our churches, people in the breach, kin in Christ, travel to this visitation at the Table of the Lord. There we are joined at this visitation by the saints of Bushasha, our companions across the church, our partners in the disaster response of comfort and renewal, those we have lost, those left behind in the breach, Mary and Elizabeth and their babies, angels and archangels and all the company of heaven in every time and every place. Here, where all roads converge, we receive the visitation of the dying and rising Christ who "set out and went with haste" to visit you and all our companions on the road. Hic. "In those days Mary set out and went with haste to a Judean town in the hill country, where she entered the house of Zechariah and greeted Elizabeth."

7. Anger to Ecstasy

"Now in Jerusalem by the Sheep Gate there is a pool, called in Hebrew Bethzatha, which has five porticos. In these lay many invalids—blind, lame, and paralyzed. One man was there who had been ill for thirty-eight years. When Jesus saw him lying there and knew that he had been there a long time, he said to him, 'Do you want to be made well?' The sick man answered him, 'Sir, I have no one to put me into the pool when the water is stirred up; and while I am making my way, someone else steps down ahead of me.' Jesus said to him, 'Stand up, take your mat and walk.'"

—John 5:2-8

Anger

"In these lay many invalids—blind, lame, and paralyzed. One man was there who had been ill for thirty-eight years." This is the chapter on tough love. Initially our hearts were broken open. After the adrenaline rush of magnificent response to disaster comes the spiritual and psychic enervation of those who settle into the new reality after tragedy. Our hearts begin to close. We stare into the abyss. I have seen a diminution of spiritual capital and energy in our synod over these five years.

Strategies that get us through the night in order to survive blunt trauma become ossified into harmful patterns of behavior. We overeat, drink too much, withdraw, and make bad decisions. Fault lines become fissures. After the tragedy, congregational and personal conflicts are bitter, call processes take longer, low-grade depression palls every meeting. One third of our pastors are no longer serving in their calls. Some have left the active ministry and name the tragedy as the reason. Others leave our synod to be with family in another part of the country. Tragedy puts the heat on what was already going on before the towers fell. The Lamentations become shriller. "Is it nothing to all you who pass by?" I will never forget, about a year and a half after 9/11, how I felt when that event and the people in New York, Washington, D. C., and Pennsylvania fell out of the prayers at the Eucharist of the Conference of Bishops meeting. No mention, liturgical amnesia. The world moves on, and we are stuck. I had predicted that this tragedy would be the ten-ton gorilla lurking in the corner of every liturgy, pastoral act. It is still true today. And beneath it all is an anger that simmers, igniting too often into conflagrations we can hardly explain. What I am describing is the process we call mourning. Our hearts need to be broken open once more. We need to move . . . not on . . . but out . . . outside ourselves, out toward the greater pain of the world.

Once upon a time Jesus showed up at the hour of worship in Jerusalem. At that place is a pool called Bethesda and in the narthex lay many invalids on their mats . . . blind, lame, paralyzed. It was a kind of Darwinian system of health care: those with the means, with the help, with the right connections, resources, friends got to the pool. One had been lying there on his mat for thirty-eight years, in sight of the healing pool but always a day late and a dollar short.

"When Jesus saw him lying there and knew that he had been there a long time, he said to him, 'Do you want to be made well?' Jesus notices the suffering and helplessness. He shows up at the place of deepest vulnerability. There are echoes of the voice speaking to Moses from the bush: "for I have seen the affliction of my people—I know their suffering." God has noticed the suffering in our many tragedies. God wants to be in the breach with us.

But why did Jesus ask the question he asked? He stands before someone chronically ill, lame and unable to walk for thirty-eight years. "Do you want to be made well?" Why ask a cripple that? It sounds insensitive, almost like a taunt. You can almost hear him grumble to himself, "Well, what do you think, J. C.?" The question rouses the man to a spirited response. He was just lying there, but now he is animated, ticked. He spits out his anger: "Sir, I have no one to put me into the pool when the water is stirred up; and while I am making my way, someone else steps down ahead of me."

Why, indeed, would Jesus ask this man that question: "Do you want to be made well?" Yet it is the only question that matters. If he doesn't, he will continue to make a life for himself sitting by the side of the pool. Our pathologies can domesticate us. You, sisters and brothers on your mat, do you want to be made well? It's the only question for congregations stalled in their ministry, timid in their stewardship, lax in their discipleship, stifled in their imagination about the future, afraid of the changing communities outside their doors. It is the only question for those who have endured tragedy and resent the world moving on while they are stuck. "You, heart closed, turned inward, still seething, paralyzed by what happened. Do you really want it? Do you want to be made well?" It's the only question for a world paralyzed by anger, sitting beside the pool on the mat of its many divisions. Do you really want it? Individually, in our congregations, our relationships, do we really want to be made well or will we clutch our rationalizations, our fears, our addictions, our self-delusions and self-absorption and talk about why we never get to the pool? Will we stop trying to drag ourselves to the pool we know we will never reach long enough to notice the healer standing in our midst?

"Jesus said to him, 'Stand up, take your mat and walk.'" Jesus does not touch him or put him in the water. Even the word for "rise" in the Greek is a reflexive verb. You can't raise someone else; you can only raise yourself. The man by the pool was caught in a thirty-eight-year cycle of apathy and anger. The root meaning for the Norse word *angr* is grief. It is mourning the distance between what was . . . and what has become; it is grief over the distance between what is . . . and what ought to be. Jesus found a man crippled in more ways than one—apathetic (*a-pathos*, without feeling). His question stirred him to grieving anger. We will never move into our many tragedies in ways that heal and serve until we get in touch with our anger and shout it out in exorcising grief. We need to unleash the lamentations stuck in our throats:

ॐ This is supposed to be a place of healing and no one helps me!

ॐ For thirty-eight damn years nobody who made it to the pool came back to help me!

ॐ People pushed me away, ran over me!

ॐ I didn't ask to be born this way; why will no one welcome me to the healing pool?

ॐ Where was God on September 11?

ॐ Why did God take my buddy in the firehouse and leave me?

ॐ Why were the poor and black and aged and disabled left behind in New Orleans?

Our lives and our life together is riddled with grieving anger between what was . . . and what has become; between what is . . . and what ought to be.

ॐ "This is my father's house and you have made it a den of thieves."

ॐ Our country welcomed my grandparents, and today we not only hate the stranger—we blame them.

ॐ In the church the only document you need is your baptismal certificate, yet if we do not demand other documents we become felons.

This kind of anger will move our values. This kind of anger will break our hearts open again. God can work with this kind of grief. Do you want to be made well? Then stand up! Get up!

But then Jesus does something else which jars us. Once the man has stood up, he is finally free to walk after thirty-eight years, he is about to take the first step into unencumbered freedom. . . . And Jesus says, "take up your mat." Jesus makes him take up his mat. In some translations he makes the man put the mat on his back. Why? Well, why do you think someone who hasn't taken a drink for ten years still calls himself an alcoholic? Why can't a person live one day at a time without a sponsor with a mat hitched to her back? Jesus rose on Easter with wounds he could show Thomas. In the story the healing by the pool led to testimony. The mat became his history in God's healing providence. Hook up your hope with your history. Those who are healed have a story to tell. The call to healing is a call not to leave our mats behind or pretend they are not there. Moses approached the burning bush in the wilderness with a mat strapped to his back. It's why God could use him. I was dragging a mat on my back in the camps in Ramallah and with the shariah judge.

The call to healing does not make light of the divisions amongst us, of what we have been through, of what we have lost. It is a call to walk away from apathy and also from hot anger. It is a call to cool *angr*, the grief of the gulf between what was and what has become; between what is and what should be. It is a holy longing to be well, a resolve to turn our gaze from the pool reflecting back our paralysis and apathy and look into the eyes of Jesus standing with us in the breach. Jesus, the one who calls us to the place of anger transformed to healing grace for the life of the world.

Ecstacy

Peter went up on the roof to pray. He became hungry and wanted something to eat; and while it was being prepared, he fell into a *trance*. He saw the heaven opened and something like a large sheet coming down being lowered to the ground by its four corners. In it were all kinds of four-footed creatures and reptiles and birds of the air. Then he heard a voice saying, "Get up, Peter; kill and eat." But Peter said, "By no means, Lord; for I have never eaten anything that is profane or unclean." The voice said to him again, a second time, "What God has made clean, you must not call profane." . . . Then Peter began to speak [to Cornelius], "I truly understand that God shows no partiality, but in every nation anyone who fears him and does what is right is acceptable to him" (Acts 10:9-15, 34).

Long before The Drifters sang about it, people have been going up on the roof for rest, refreshment, and escape. Peter was in the home of Simon the tanner in the city of Joppa in the early Pentecost days of the church. He goes up on the roof to wait for lunch. He goes into a trance.

Up the coast in Caesarea, Cornelius, a Roman general and a Gentile, is also hungry. He is seeking God. He sends for Peter, whose fame as a spiritual leader is growing rapidly. Will Peter, a Jew, come to see this Gentile spiritual seeker? Cornelius wants to know if the God of Peter and Abraham and Sarah and Isaac also loves Gentiles.

In his trance Peter sees all kinds of food descend on a tablecloth. He is hungry, but the food is not kosher. He would dishonor God by eating what is ritually unclean. God speaks. "If I make something clean, it is truly clean." "Bon appétit." Strangers knock on the door. Peter comes out of his trance. Messengers from Gentile Cornelius want Peter to come with them and teach them about the true God. Peter goes. In the living room of a Gentile in Caesarea the first words out of Peter's mouth are these: "God doesn't play favorites. Everyone is acceptable to God."

This remarkable story of God's grace crossing boundaries turns on the "trance" of Peter the daydreamer on the roof. The English word *trance* is inadequate, suggesting a kind of woozy reverie. The Greek word for trance is *ek-stasis*, a dynamic word from which we get the word *ecstasy*. *Ekstasis* means, literally, "to step forth." It is the shift in consciousness of Peter, hungry on a rooftop, who in a moment of "ekstasis" was made vulnerable to the imagery of the sheet full of animals, unclean as well as clean. The insight about God's inclusion of the Gentiles, which had been repressed and resisted by his everyday consciousness and worldview, overwhelmed him in the state of openness and receptivity that is ecstasy, *ekstasis*. For Luke, "ecstasy" is the business of the Holy Spirit.

How can we heal from the tragedies of our lives which tend to immobilize us, to cause us to hunker down in the safe, the familiar, mired in despair and anger? Jesus drew out the man by the pool to name his anger and cry out his lament, moving him to *ekstasis,* a stepping out of his pathological rut and into the ecstasy of walking wounded back into the world, his mat on his back. Healing begins with the hunger for ecstasy, for the kind of experience that is open to the urgent interior word of the living Christ who dwells in each of us. Life in Christ asks us to step out continually into wider worlds, deeper spiritual insights, passionate engagement with the calling each of us has from God. What will it take to get us thinking and acting outside of ourselves, our undercrofts, our worldviews, our tragedies, our narrow spiritual horizons? We live in a culture of too many trances and reveries that are only celebrations of the self or of a received tradition. We are Balkanized, walled off from one another. And there comes a time in the cycle of a tragedy or disaster when our response is to retreat into enclaves we think will keep us safe.

That is what happened after September 11 in America. We tightened our borders. We hunted and harassed immigrants among us. Our leaders played on our fears and led us into war, enclave

America going it alone. Too often religion blessed it. We rendered to Caesar everything belonging to Caesar *and to God*. In our anger we remained stuck at Ground Zero, living in a hall of mirrors.

True movement from anger to ecstasy is controversial, because ecstasy means leaving the usual and safe behind. After baptizing the Gentile, Cornelius, and his household, Peter had some explaining to do back at the bishop's office at synod headquarters in Jerusalem.

Ecstatic Disaster Response

The New Testament was written in the shadow of tragedy and disaster. The persecution of those who followed Jesus propelled the Jesus movement out into the wider world, especially when the messianic party was expelled from the temple.

The destruction of the temple in Jerusalem by the Romans in 70 A.D. was the Ground Zero of that era. Some despaired, wondering whether God's promises had failed. But two forms of Israel's faith survived, disbursed in the empire. The Pharasaic school which had been forged in the synagogues following the first destruction became the Rabbinic Judaism of the Second Century. The followers of Messiah Jesus became the Christian movement, dominantly Gentile by mid-Second Century. Both traditions embodied the Scriptures. In his Hien Fry seminary lecture, David Tiede contrasts the ecstatic outreach to the Gentiles of Peter and Paul with the life and message of the Risen Christ, to the Avoth in the rabbinic Mishnah.

Moses received the Law from Sinai and handed it down to Joshua, and Joshua to the elders and the elders to the prophets, and the prophets handed it down to the men of the Great Assembly. They said three things: Be deliberate in judgment, raise up many disciples, and make a fence around the Torah.

The rabbis had an enclave strategy to keep Israel faithful when the world comes apart, which conserved Diaspora communities for centuries.

Be deliberate in judgment. The community must be preserved and protected from ecstasy.

Raise up many disciples. Israel's enclave faith is more a matter of teaching and learning than acting and telling and reaching out.

Make a fence around the Torah. Israel's faith and practice must be purified and protected from contamination. If all Israel were to keep Torah for one day, Messiah will come. Israel is God's enclave of holiness on earth.

The story of the book of Acts is how the messianic message of Israel's faith in the crucified and risen Lord burst the enclave. The Apostles of Jesus fanned out to the network of synagogues throughout Asia Minor, Greece, North Africa, Italy. The news could not stay inside the synagogues. Luke lays claim to Israel's prophetic hope from the time of the first exile. When Isaiah was called to gather Israel to return to God, God gave a yet more profound commission, a Great Commission: "It is too light a thing that you should be my servant to raise up the tribes of Jacob and to restore the survivors of Israel: [restoration is good, but not enough!] I will give you as a light to the nations, that my salvation may reach to the end of the earth" (Isaiah 49:6). Luke through Acts is the story of how God turned Israel outside of preserving itself into an instrument of God's saving light for the nations of the world. It is a disaster response still active in the world.

The Long Mourner's Bench

Five years after September 11, 2001, is a time to remember that our insularity, security, and narrow view of life was pierced, perhaps forever. Our life changed, our world view changed. I hope that as we heal we are moving from anger to ecstasy, more compassionate, more in tune with suffering around the world. Ground Zero opened up a global window. In many ways these past years of war, terror, and national hubris have also slammed shut many of these windows. These years also have linked us to many other names: Darfur, Kabul, Baghdad, Madrid, Beslan, London, Niger, Haifa, Jerusalem, Ramallah, Beirut, New Orleans, the Gulf Coast, hurricane alley in Florida, the South Asian seacoast. May our hearts break open once again. Richard John Neuhaus shares a beautiful quote by Peter de Vries in an article he wrote on illness and health. With our mats on our backs let the re-enchantment of our spiritual selves help us recognize, in the words of Peter de Vries in "The Blood of the Lamb":

"the recognition of how long, how very long, is the mourners' bench upon which we sit, arms linked in undeluded friendship—all of us, brief links ourselves, in the eternal pity."

Can we see each of our congregations as links on the long mourners' bench? As we step forth from "church usual" in ecstasy we are linked to places of hurt and hope around the world. Let us find ourselves on the long mourners' bench with a renewed understanding that the only true security in this world is at the baptismal font and in the well-being of every child of God in the world, especially the poor and vulnerable.

The long mourners' bench reminds us that recovery from terror, war, disaster is a marathon, not a sprint. The poor are poorer here in New York since 9/11, the stranger is even more sidelined and despised, our disaster relief efforts are still addressing the wave effects of our common tragedy five years ago, meeting need that is in some ways more acute than ever. Because, you see, we are supposed to get over it and move on. But I am remembering the forty-seven children in our schools who lost parents, the many funerals and memorials done in our churches, those so traumatized they still cannot leave their homes. The "empty sky" downtown of the Bruce Springsteen song will not let us forget. Our short attention span in this culture has already let go of our sisters and brothers whose lives were torn apart in the South Asian tsunamis. The death of school children in Beslan is now just a picture of angry mothers meeting with Vladimir Putin on the back page. Last year's hurricane victims or last month's victims of Midwest tornados are already beside the point.

But the mourners' bench is long, and God's attention is infinite. The one who remembers the sparrow is the one who reached out to a cripple by a pool, a leader having ecstatic visions on a roof, the one who calls us to sink again into the "eternal pity," to our solidarity with all who suffer. We must not look away and we must never forget. The church is God's reminder that suffering is never isolated, meaningless, anonymous, but always linked to the long mourner's bench upon which we sit, arms linked in undiluted friendship, and linked forever to the cross and resurrection of Jesus.

From Ground Zero Outward

The Ground Zero of every tragedy connects to the long mourner's bench. On September 11 the point of impact was downtown, but the whole metropolis was broken, wounded, filled with tears. And September 11 only deepened what had been going on in New York for a long time.

At Ground Zero when the remains of a child of God were found something remarkable would happen. All activity would cease. The pile would gentle down to silence. With bowed, uncovered heads everyone at Ground Zero would show their consummate respect for life as the remains would be lovingly brought out from the rubble. Then all of the concerted effort, first for rescue, then for recovery, would again resume.

Think of the Ground Zeros we have missed, and those we have yet to address. Can we see the same reverent respect for life, and the same sheer effort at rescue and recovery for people with AIDS and their loved ones? For neighborhoods where the vision for rebuilding is to spend more for jails than for schools? For the stranger among us now hunted and blamed and subject to extra legal detentions? For the economic victims who never had anyone give them a thousand-dollar-a-plate dinner: the undocumented, the Fujianese sweatshop worker in Chinatown; the domestics and limo drivers, the window washers and food stall vendors; the homeless who might find a bed in a Bronx jail.

Tragedy is a time to call public officials to the long mourner's bench. That is the meta-question in New Orleans these days after Katrina. Will *all* of the city be rebuilt and renewed? Can we extend the holy respect for life and heroic effort of Ground Zero and all of our disaster responses to our entire cities and places of hurt and hope throughout the world?

Madrid

The New York interfaith community and its leaders gathered with Spanish leaders and residents of New York at St. Paul's Chapel near Ground Zero on the third anniversary of 9/11. The mourner's bench was lengthening out beyond what happened in New York. A cellist played a haunting and beautiful sonata by Pablo Casals. There were prayers, music, and remembrance. From the chapel we walked together to Ground Zero for silence and more prayers.

At the gathering I read a text from Isaiah. "Upon your walls, O Jerusalem, I have posted sentinels; all day and all night they shall never be silent. You, who remind the Lord, take no rest . . . and you shall be called, 'Sought Out, A City Not Forsaken'" (Isaiah 62:6, 12).

I remembered what happened that day, on March 11, 2003, 7:39 A.M.: the first of ten bombs blow apart four trains carrying commuters from western Madrid to the Atocha train station in the city center. The force of the blasts rips gaping holes in the trains. Ambulances race to the scene, makeshift first-aid centers are set up, and local hospitals are quickly flooded with victims and their families. Passengers and passersby help rescue the injured, while hundreds respond to an urgent appeal for blood donors. Truly, we in New York have lived out those details in a scene of terror. We remember a bright, beautiful September morning when, like in

Madrid, we began the routine of our day, ascended and descended to the trains which carry us to buildings in which we work.

And I said this to our Spanish guests, "We want you to know that we remember. We saw your candles in the rain, 2.3 million of you in Madrid, on the Friday after the attacks on your city. We felt your resolve to protest these attacks and to embrace one another in comfort and solidarity. And we remember. As we staggered from the attacks on our city, when we did not know if we could bear it, we saw your candles in the days after September 11, millions of candles in Madrid, Barcelona, across your country. You reached out to us, with millions from around the world. We have not forgotten. Please know now that this memorial service is a candle from the interfaith community of New York, shining brightly for you. It shines in gratitude, for we have not forgotten that you did not leave us alone after the attacks on our city. We want you to know that you are not alone as you begin to remember each year what happened to you and how your world changed.

"We are praying for you. We know that the everyday experience of getting on a commuter train in the morning will never again be the same for you. We are praying for the comfort of God as you continue to mourn your dead. We are praying for your city and especially for those who are poor or immigrant, for we know how terror can lead us to distrust the stranger and how its effects hurt the most vulnerable. We are praying for your religious leaders and institutions, and for people of faith throughout your city, for we have learned how spiritually vulnerable and hungry we have all become as we seek security and comfort and meaning in the midst of tragedy. May you be strengthened by God and by your faith to offer yourselves to the city as signs of hope.

"Terror and violence have thrust us into community with one another. That community tragically continues to lengthen as we now together must express our solidarity with our sisters and brothers in Beslan, Russia, as they bury their children. We must together seek community with all who have learned only too well the human cost of violence for the dead and the living.

We must find a way to find each other, to find our collective voices around the world, to shout NO! to the way of violence and terror. And we must also find our collective resolve to call the world to a realization that the only true security in this world rests in the well being, safety, and dignity of every human being. And we must offer collectively the compassion which comes from the God whose presence sustains us when the towers fall, the trains explode, and the school goes up in flames.

"From New York to Madrid, we remind you that you shall be called, 'Sought Out, A City Not Forsaken.'"

Tsunami

With lit candles we gathered at St. Paul's International Church after the South Asian Tsunami to comfort one another and pray for the victims and their families. The liturgy was planned and hosted by the south Asian ministry of our synod. We watched images on a large screen of the devastation and suffering. Brothers and sisters from India, Sri Lanka, Indonesia, and Taiwan testified eloquently to the great sadness through tears and prayers. Some had been there. All were in touch with the stories, had lost loved ones. We sang "Sarenam, Sarenam" as we did in the days after 9/11, which means "refuge" in Sanskrit, and we took refuge in one another.

Jesus, Savior, Lord, Lo to you I fly
Sarenam, Sarenam, Sarenam
You the rock,
My refuge higher that I
Sarenam, Sarenam, Sarenam.

(Words: Trad. Pakistani; trans. by D. T. Niles, 1963; Music: Trad. Punjabi melody; arr. By Shanti Rasanayagam, 1962; Trans. and arr. by permission of Christian Conference of Asia)

Refugees

Bethlehem: Over two thousand people are crammed into the warren of alleys and decrepit housing of the A'ida refugee camp in Bethlehem. I have experienced places of poverty around the world, but there was an air of claustrophobic hopelessness I had never seen before. Images paint the picture:

- The only clinic is shut and abandoned.
- An Israeli army post stands at the end of a garbage-strewn street, which also guards Rachel's tomb.
- There is a cluster of the little shacks which were the original housing built by the U. N. in 1948.
- A library provides relief from the relentless bleakness of the place. It has an Internet connection and books of spiritual and psychological uplift for children.
- On a store window is a picture of a young man shot and killed while throwing stones. There is a wall of pictures ("martyrs"), one is the picture of a father of six children killed trying to collect his kids. Two months later his brother was killed. Our two guides are brothers who have been living in the camp all their lives. They tell us thirty-five have been killed in this camp since the current intifada began.
- A concrete structure holds cement and construction materials. It is part of a micro enterprise program for those who want to build a wall or a room. Most people in the camp were laborers in Jerusalem and all are unemployed.
- We walk through the narrow alleys, past walls strewn with graffiti and bullet holes. The Israeli soldiers were afraid of these alleys so they made holes in the walls of contiguous homes to get from home to home.
- At the head of the alley is a church and a mosque. Three nuns died of heart attacks during one battle.
- People are curious and gracious. They are glad we are here and want to get their story out. A little boy follows us dragging

an improvised toy (a slab of cardboard tied to a scrap of material) through the dust.

↜ Up ahead is a school with a blue U. N. sign on the roof. Its walls are pockmarked with bullet holes—the shooting happened while the children were in school.

↜ Green Italian signs indicate their help in repairing some of the damage. A mosque has been reduced to rubble. On a standing wall are pictures of young men and boys with guns.

↜ At the perimeter of the camp is rubble-strewn property owned by the Armenian Church. The Israelis built a dividing wall. Across from the wall is a line of homes. Every lower level is littered with broken glass and is uninhabitable. We are told that every home in the camp has a prisoner or a martyr. Most homes have a child who has been harmed. Muslims and Christians have worked together, sharing food, shelter, and consolation. Our guides pointed out Christian and Moslem homes.

↜ We went to a dwelling on one of the alleys where an old man greeted us. His sons had been our guides. Gracious hospitality among Palestinians is habitual and primal. We shared the heat of the day and tea and cold drinks with our hosts. He swept his hand over the brutal landscape of the camp when the talk came to terrorism: "This is what we are driven to." He came to the camp in 1948. He spoke wistfully of his home village near Beit Shemesh. The "right of return" for refugees is a non-starter with every Israeli we talked to, even the most irenic. This man spoke of the biblical concept of Jubilee. "If we are brothers let us share the land."

Jerusalem

We spoke with a leader of the Shinui, a party which advocates peace, and limiting the power of religious parties. His father had walked from Tehran to the Wailing Wall one hundred fifty years ago. Forty years ago he had walked into Notre Dame during conflict. But this did not make him a fervid nationalist. He wants peace and justice in the holy land. Israeli high school kids go to Poland to concentration camps as part of their curriculum. This often makes them militaristic with a desire for revenge. His mother, a survivor of the camps, always wanted to make sure her children had "the right conclusion" concerning such visits. Never treat others without justice and dignity. He believes that Israelis themselves are being hurt by the way they are treating Palestinians. His party went from five to fifteen members in the Knesset. Five of the twelve positive votes on the "road map" for peace came from his party. And yet, "when I stand next to a place where suicide bombing happened I am confused. . . ."

Home

The wing of the plane tips low toward the jumble of Tel Aviv and the blue Mediterranean. Down there are the camps and schools and hospitals we had visited. Busses and cars move like tiny ants. Friday prayers on the temple mount at El Aqsa Mosque will begin in a few hours, then in the evening Sabbath will again approach the faithful as a lover. On Sunday morning the bells of Redeemer Lutheran Church will again ring out in the Old City. The rocks and hills and living stones begin to disappear. The intensely local recedes, dissolves into a birds-eye view. Below us now is only the water as we climb up and away from the holy land. As the engines drone, hurtling me toward the holy land of New York I pray this psalm:

"Pray for the peace of Jerusalem: 'May they prosper who love you. Peace be within your walls, and security within your towers.' For the sake of my relatives and friends I will say, 'Peace be within you.' For the sake of the house of the Lord our God, I will seek your good" (Psalm 122:6-9).

Shock and Awe . . . Righteousness and Peace

One of our responses to the 9/11 attacks was to form a Center for Public Theology to address the issues on the long mourner's bench. One of our trustees had co-produced the movie *The Milagro Beanfield War*, and then was an Emmy-award-winning television programmer. When the war in Iraq broke out he was able to turn out the press at a "Mass for Peace" at St. Peter's in midtown. They televised parts of the service, the sermon, as well as interviews. The words I spoke that night were spoken with a mat on my back, seeking a place on the long mourner's bench. "Steadfast love and faithfulness will meet; righteousness and peace will kiss each other" (Psalm 85:10).

Shock and awe. Shock is what we are feeling the world over at this war that has proceeded inexorably from the ashes and continuing pain of the September 11 shock. We are shocked that we just quit talking and began fighting. Shocked at finding ourselves pretty much alone in the family of nations, having decided to go it our own way. Shocked because we in this city know too well what happens to buildings and those in them as explosives hit them and they are ground to concrete and human dust. There are people in those bright flashes beaming into our bedrooms in this television war. I am haunted when I speak to Pastor Khader El Yateem and hear about our fellow Lutherans at Salam Lutheran Church who are from Baghdad, and how they yearn for news of loved ones. "Collateral damage" could include loved faces, human hearts of people very close to us. And yes, shock is the controlling emotion evoked by the precision and implacable advance of the war machine as it envelops Iraq. Our shock includes images of prisoners of war, mounting casualties, communal discord which reminds me of the Viet Nam war. I have spoken to pastors called to military duty, walking with them as they absorb with their families and congregations the shock of leaving for a year's duty. Maybe most shocking of all is that we have once again become spectators to the destruction of human life, accepted body counts that place a higher value on some lives than on others. Shocked that our communal tragedy of September 11 has been used as a reason to unleash this campaign of "shock and awe," in the face of these words from the

Prince of Peace: "Bless those who persecute you . . . love your enemies."

We stand in a long line of those who have been shocked by war and the venality of affairs among nations. In biblical times when Israel forgot that it was blessed to be a blessing to all the nations, when it threw its weight around like all the other nations, when its highest priority was not the welfare of the most vulnerable of its citizens and the stranger among them, then they received the shock of the withdrawal of God's favor. From our Psalm, "Will you be angry with us forever? Will you prolong your anger to all generations? Will you not revive us life again, so that your people may rejoice in you?" (Psalm 85:5, 6).

Shock and awe. Yes, this war can provoke shock among us. But awe belongs to God. "Be still and know that I am God." "Render to Caesar what is Caesar's, and to God what is God's." I will render shock to Caesar, but I stand in awe of God, the creator of all things.

"Show us your steadfast love, O Lord, and grant us your salvation. Let me hear what God the Lord God will speak, for he will speak peace to his people, to his faithful, to those who turn to him in their hearts" (Psalm 85:7, 8). I call on all who stand in awe of God, from whatever your spiritual journey and tradition, to love your enemy, whether you perceive that enemy to be Iraq, or those who are pursuing this war. It is time for listening, to God and one another. It is too easy to claim the moral high ground and rule out those who disagree. People who love their country find themselves with differing views and conclusions. We must all resist the arrogance and smugness that shuts down conversation. These events are complex, resistant of bumper sticker solutions.

We must pray for and support those who have been placed in harm's way by this war—the courageous men and women serving in the military and those chaplains who serve them on our behalf. One of our pastors, an air force chaplain, writes: "We are very busy here, lots of planes, and soldiers and equipment flowing through, young kids . . . man! Not much older than Joseph [his son]. The hardest visit was a young female airman boarding the bus to take her out to the plane. She was crying. . . . I went up and talked with her. 'Your first deployment?' She said, 'Yes, but that is not why I am crying.' She was leaving her seven-month-old daughter behind at home, her firstborn! Yes, a changing face of war, needless to say my heart wept for her."

We must pray for the lives and hearts of their opponents, whom Saddam has placed in harm's way. We must pray for and show hospitality to the stranger among us, especially immigrants from Muslim and Arab-speaking countries. Ghassan Dauod, a case manager for Project Life of Lutheran Social Services writes: "Thank you for your heartfelt statement on the beginning of this war. . . . As an Arab and Muslim-American, I publicly condemned the attack on September 11. I think those who committed this crime tried to rob our faith and culture as Arab-Americans. . . . With the same conviction I condemn the destruction of any other city and the killing of innocent people around the world. I pray for the destruction to stop, and that peace will prevail around the world." We must have a public conversation with includes Ghassan Daoud and our chaplains called to active duty.

"Let me hear what God the Lord is saying . . ." We must listen together to what the Lord is saying, and we must listen very carefully to one another. What has been especially shocking to me is that no alternative vision is emerging. We stopped talking. We went to war. Some support it. Some oppose it. But where is the war of ideas, of a positive view of the world in which we can unite, which can capture the best of our spiritual traditions and disciplines? We have public conflict. Where is public theology? Where in the public arena is space to be still, to go deep in our faith, to stand in awe before God and one another, and with the apostle Paul to say, "Let me show you a better way. . . . If I speak in the tongues of mortals and of angels, but do not have love, I am a noisy gong or a clanging cymbal" (1 Cor. 13:1).

Paul Berman in *New York Times Magazine* writes: "It would be nice to think that, in the war against terror, our side, too, speaks of deep philosophical ideas . . . but we speak of what? . . . United Nations resolutions, of unilateralism, of multilateralism, of weapons inspectors, of coercion and non coercion. This is no answer to the terrorists. The terrorist speak insanely of deep things . . . but who will speak of the sacred and the secular, of the physical world and the spiritual world? Armies are in motion, but are the philosophers and religious leaders likewise in motion?"

There is, of course, an alternative vision, and it rises from the awe of the presence of the God of history. "Steadfast love and faithfulness will meet; righteousness and peace will kiss each other. Faithfulness will spring up from the ground, and righteousness will look down from the sky. . . . Righteousness will go before him, and will make a path for his steps" (Psalm 85:10, 11, 13). Righteousness and peace. In Hebrew scripture the term *mishpat* means "justice" in the sense that it is the exercise of power, the rendering of the values of the community. But this "mishpat" comes out of a consensus, or mythos which holds a community together, a sense of what is right, "sedeq," which we have come to call *righteousness*. There were two competing notions of sedeq. The Cannanite myths which rendered the "mishpat" of Baal supreme came out of a consensus, or "sedeq" of survival. On the margins of that society in the twelfth century B.C., a new consensus emerged with the appearance of the "a'piru" (Hebrews, literally, "those on the margins"). What formed them as a people was the acceptance of the "sedeq" of Yahweh, the God who hears the cry of the oppressed and delivers them from the hand of the oppressor. It is the righteousness of remembering those on the margins, the orphan, the widow, the stranger. Thus we had, and continue to have, two contradictory notions of "sedeq," righteousness: bread or justice, survival or servant love, a sense of abundance or scarcity, life or death, Baal or God.

We need a public conversation about the righteousness that must kiss peace. We need to speak truthfully with one another about how to wage peace with righteousness in a city still in shock from 9/11: where food banks are going empty, jobs are more scarce than ever, our immigrant neighbors are fearful, health care for those on the margins is collapsing in state and federal budgets. As the war continues we must offer fervent prayer and constant anchoring in the sources of our spiritual heritages that describe the relationship between citizenship and faith, righteousness and peace, love and justice.

Shock and awe. Righteousness and peace. So come to the communion table now. Here righteousness and peace kiss one another in the presence of God. Here everyone eats. Here all are welcome. Here everyone communes with God and one another, with our loved ones in harm's way, with those who have died in this conflict and all who have gone before us, with angels and archangels and all the company of heaven, in every time and place. Here public theology becomes a matter of eating and drinking with one another in love and hope. And for the Christian, standing in the midst of this meal is the dying and rising Christ. Here is gratitude, Eucharist. "Lord, you were favorable to your land; you restored the fortunes of Jacob. . . . Righteousness will go before him, and will make a path for his steps" (Psalm 85:1, 13).

Bishop Stephen Paul Bouman
Saint Peter's Church, New York City, Lent 3
March 2003

8. Cruciform Rising

"Do you not know that all of us who have been baptized into Christ Jesus were baptized into his death? Therefore we have been buried with him by baptism into death, so that, just as Christ was raised from the dead by the glory of the Father, so we too might walk in newness of life. For if we have united with him in a death like his, we will certainly be united with him in a resurrection like his."

—Romans 6:3-5

Nina's Question

When visiting our son in the Peace Corps in Ukraine we met a wonderful woman named Nina. She taught with our son, and her husband had been an officer in the Soviet Army. Things were tough economically for everyone. "It's our reality," she would shrug as she spoke of long bread lines, no jobs, electricity blackouts, rising crime. She was raised on Soviet atheism and taught to be cynical of any sign of religious faith. She knew I was a pastor. She had sized me up and apparently decided I was not a religious fanatic or someone who would fall for irrational answers to deep questions. One day she looked at me and said, "Really, I mean really. Do you really believe all this religious stuff? Really! What do you believe? Do you really think there is more after death? I mean really!" That is the question, isn't it?

I brought Nina's question to Ground Zero with me. At that hellish place for the first time, breathing lightly through my mask to avoid the sweet smell of the death of my sisters and brothers, the furious grinding of gears and metal of the rescue effort all around me, I contemplated the obscene rubble and groped for something, anything to give me consolation. I had pictures in my mind of those I knew were buried in that mess. There is no happy little ending one can tack onto that. But a memory came to me as a gift. My grandfather, a pastor and seminary teacher of New Testament, was fishing with me when I was about eight years old. He looked at me and said: "Stephen, the only death you have to be afraid of is already behind you in your baptism." And then he went on fishing. He was with me at the pile as I remembered my baptismal answer to Nina's question.

We have already been buried alive. "Do you not know that all of us who have been baptized into Christ Jesus were baptized into his death? Therefore we have been buried with him by baptism into death, so that, just as Christ was raised from the dead by the glory of the Father, so we too might walk in newness of life. For if we have united with him in a death like his, we will certainly be united with him in a resurrection like his" (Romans 6:3-5).

Tragedy causes us to question and speak of ultimate things even when there are no proximate answers.

The End of the Story

On March 10, 2002, six months after the September 11 attacks, there was a television special on the firefighters. The filmmakers were working on a documentary of life inside a fire house. I was haunted as I watched them begin their day, the male camaraderie and joshing inside the house, the devotion to duty overlaid with boredom, the morning coffee and bagels, the quotidian gestures and conversation. But we knew what was waiting for them. It gave weight to every facial expression, every gesture, and every breath they took. We breathed with them the unbearable heaviness of being. It was heartbreaking to watch them race to the towers, then see them gather in the lobby because we knew they were planning and groping and rescuing in what would be the tomb of so many of them. Close by, the thud of falling bodies. Chaplain Michael Judge, his face a knot of concern. Then blackness. Then we saw his broken body gently and reverently laid on the altar of old St. Peter's, and we knew how many more would be borne up from the rubble.

Sören Kierkegaard said that purity of spirit is to will one thing. Many intellectual, cultural, and theological eddies and streams flow out of the great river of the church, but one strong, inexorable current feeds them all. The resurrection of Jesus from the dead is the Ground Zero of human history and cosmic existence. My cousin, Walter Bouman, a teacher for many years at Trinity Seminary in Columbus, Ohio, read human history the way he read detective novels, by reading the last chapter first. He knew, we know, the ending! And it gives weight to every moment.

Like watching doomed firefighters living out their lives in the shadow of Ground Zero, the Christian lives out of the knowledge of the paschal mystery. We know how it all turned out, how it will all turn out. This knowledge of the empty tomb gives a weight to our everyday lives and ministry as well. The Ground Zero of the resurrection of Jesus from the dead looms over our every thought, song, gesture, ministry, and disaster response. It adds weight to our response to tragedy, and to every moment on our own homeward way. I said at Walter's funeral, "Knowing the end of the story means that we are laying to rest a conqueror today."

"In all these things we are more than conquerors through him who loved us. For I am convinced that neither death, nor life . . . will be able to separate us from the love of God in Christ Jesus our Lord."

—Romans 8:37-39

Blinded by the Light

St. Paul was stunned by the resurrection of Jesus and never got over it. Paul experienced the resurrection of Jesus as both conversion and commissioning for ministry. I have been reflecting recently on Caravaggio's painting of the scene of the road to Damascus. Paul is flat on his back. Legs outstretched, arms raised up to heaven as he falls, his eyes shut since he has been blinded by the resurrection light. The central figure in the painting is the horse, which is shown sensitively lifting its hoof so as not to tread on the poor, vulnerable creature sprawled beneath it. Paul knew and taught that to follow Jesus, to live the baptismal adventure, is to be utterly dependent on grace, always ready to be broken again by encounter with the truth, unprotected, needy.

If Jesus beckons us beyond death, the future is open and hope and promise are possible. The Reformation is a pastoral call to get the end of the story right, to be vulnerable to the future beyond death, to give up death-denying justifications, to be placed by baptism into the death and resurrection of Jesus.

The resurrection of Jesus animates how we read and interpret the Bible. Scripture is indispensable for the church because it gives us the narratives of Israel, the cross and resurrection of Jesus, the birth of the church. "Were not our hearts burning within us . . . ?" Is it any wonder, then, that in tragedy the Bible comes alive, that Nina's question is given a narrative of hope, that we are re-enchanted by the resurrection?

The Community of the Resurrection

God's most gracious response to the tragedy of human history is the church, the community of the Resurrection. Think of your home congregation, or of one you remember. People attend churches for many reasons—but why do they persist in bringing themselves and their babies to the baptismal font? Why do they keep showing up? At the heart of the matter is Nina's question.

The church must speak its own truth, in season and out. Ultimate security will never be found in this world—we all will die. We bring our children and ourselves to the baptismal font because at the end of the day it is there that Nina's question is answered. We place ourselves and our loved ones into the only secure place in this universe, into the arms of Jesus who has promised that in his death and resurrection not even death can separate us from the love of God. The congregation answers Nina's question.

What We Do

We had just returned home from a family vacation in Maine. It was evening; the phone rang. Dorothy said, "Carmine collapsed. We are at the emergency room at Holy Name. Please come." Dorothy and Carmine were like family to us, members of the congregation. As I was leaving, putting on a black shirt and collar over blue jeans, our son, Timothy, maybe twelve, said, "I'll go with you, Dad."

In the waiting room were the many friends and relatives, dressed in the tuxedos and gowns worn for the fiftieth wedding anniversary of Dorothy and Carmine. I went through the doors that say, "Keep out." Carmine had just died. I went back out into the lobby. Everyone looked at me with Nina's question on his or her hearts. When there are no words, then we say the words of the church. Ministry goes out to the daily Ground Zeros of people's lives: to emergency rooms, hospital bedsides, places of death and hope and suffering, offering the words of the church which I shared in the emergency room after telling them that Carmine had died. "In my father's house are many rooms . . ." "I am the resurrection and the life . . ." "Yea, though I walk through the valley of the shadow of death . . ." We prayed, I hugged Dorothy and left, drove about one hundred yards, pulled over and put my head on the steering wheel to cry. Then I heard my son saying softly next to me. "So, Dad, that's what you do."

So, this is what we have been doing as the church in the midst of the joys and tragedies of human living. We have been answering Nina's question with the Good News of the Resurrection of Jesus from the dead. This quotidian life of a congregation is reanimated when tragedy strikes. In calling and sending out pastors into the neighborhood and emergency rooms, in ministries of education, youth ministries, the hope and meaning of the resurrection of Jesus from the dead is taught. In liturgy, baptism, Holy Communion, in creating space for lamentations, and in participating as "repairers of the breach," in all of it, the story of Jesus' victory over death at the cross and empty tomb is lived out in magnificent grace and hope.

"Why are you cast down, O my soul, and why are you disquieted within me? Hope in God; for I shall again praise him, my help and my God."

—Psalm 42:5

A Fresh Start

When I had the privilege of participating at the interfaith gathering at Abyssinian Baptist on the Thursday after September 11, I had a strong feeling of Lutheran/Baptist déjà vu. The Lutheran theologian, Dietrich Bonhoeffer, when he was teaching at Union Seminary, enjoyed worshiping at Abyssinian. His good friend Adam Clayton Powell was his counselor as Bonhoeffer made the decision to go back to Germany and help the church resist Hitler. This martyr of the church also taught catechism at Abyssinian. Here is what Bonhoeffer wrote to mark Hitler's ten years of power.

"We used to think that one of the inalienable rights of persons was that one should be able to plan both one's professional and private life. This is a thing of the past. The force of circumstances has brought us into a situation where we have to give up being 'anxious' about tomorrow (Matthew 6:34). But it makes all the difference whether we accept this willingly and in faith or under continual constraint. For most people the compulsory abandonment of planning for the future means that they are forced back into living just for the moment, irresponsibly, frivolously, or resignedly; some dream longingly of a better time to come and try to forget the present. We find both these courses equally impossible and there remains only the very narrow way, often extremely difficult to find, of living every day as if it were our last, yet living in faith and responsibility as though there were to be a great future. 'Houses and fields and vineyards shall again be bought in this land,' proclaims the prophet (Jeremiah 32:15) in paradoxical contrast to the bleakness of his time. It is a sign from God and a pledge of a fresh start and a great future, just when all seems bleak" (*Letters and Papers from Prison* [New York: MacMillan Publishing Company, 1979], 14).

When tragedy visits we endure because of God's grace all around us. Through ministries of eyewitness testimony, lamentations, re-enchantment, repairers of the breach, visitation, vocation, solidarity, God's great future comes into view, just when all seems bleak. It is called Resurrection, the beginning of the story. God's ultimate grace all around us.

Other Resources from Augsburg

God in the Raging Waters by Paul Blom
96 pages, 978-0-8066-5317-4

This book tells the story of how the Lutheran church and its people have responded to the suffering of those most affected by Hurricanes Katrina and Rita. Included are powerful firsthand accounts, insightful theological reflections, and questions for group use.

Fire of Grace by Richard Rouse
176 pages, 978-0-8066-5112-5

Trinity Lutheran Church was burned to the ground by an arsonist. When he was imprisoned, one of his first visitors was Rick Rouse, pastor of the church he burned. Pastor Rouse outlines the path toward reconciliation that many have experienced when relying upon God's gift of forgiveness.

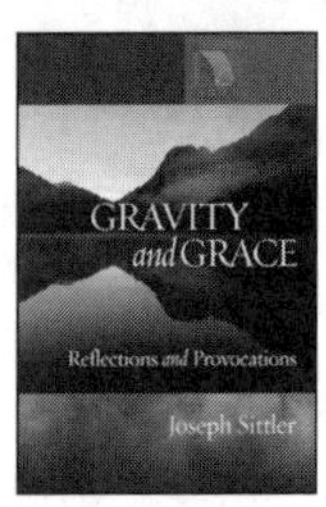

Gravity and Grace by Joseph Sittler
128 pages, 978-0-8066-5173-6

The essays and reflections gathered in this volume provoke readers to think about and discuss topics such as risk and faith, nature and grace, the Word of God and genuine theology, real education, the beauty and meaning of language, necessary personal choices, aging, and social issues.

A Forgiving Heart edited by Lyn Klug
208 pages, 978-0-8066-3997-0

This collection of powerful prayers offers understanding and new perspectives, providing healing for our relationship with God, ourselves, family and friends, in our communities, and among nations. Gathered from spiritual writers including C.S. Lewis, Mother Teresa, Henri Nouwen, and Desmond Tutu, as well as ordinary people.

Available wherever books are sold.